G000162005

ALL ABOUT CRYSTALS
Connie Islin
ISBN 965-494-111-2

ALL ABOUT TAROT
Hali Morag
ISBN 965-494-062-0

ALL ABOUT THE WICCA OF LOVE
Tabatha Jennings
ISBN 965-494-110-4

ALL ABOUT THE SIXTH SENSE
Tom Pearson
ISBN 965-494-138-4

ALL ABOUT NUMEROLOGY
Lia Robin
ISBN 965-494-109-0

ALL ABOUT PALMISTRY
Batia Shorek
ISBN 965-494-094-9

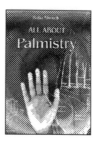

ALL ABOUT DREAMS
Eili Goldberg
ISBN 965-494-061-2

ALL ABOUT PREDICTING THE FUTURE
Sarah Zehavi
ISBN 965-494-093-0

ALL ABOUT SYMBOLS
Andrew T. Cummings
ISBN 965-494-139-2

ALL ABOUT CHAKRAS
Lily Rooman
ISBN 965-494-149-X

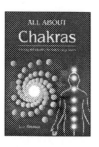

Robert Parish

ALL ABOUT
Reincarnation

Legends, Beliefs, Theories and
Personal Experiences

Astrolog Publishing House Ltd.

Cover design: Na'ama Yaffe

© Astrolog Publishing House 2004

ISBN 965-494-193-7

All rights reserved to Astrolog Publishing House Ltd.

P. O. Box 1123, Hod Hasharon 45111, Israel

Tel: 972-9-7412044

Fax: 972-9-7442714

Published by Astrolog Publishing House 2004

10 9 8 7 6 5 4 3 2 1

Contents

Introduction

Is there life after death? This question is not an easy one, especially when there are people who also ask: Is there life before death?

Despite the paradox in the question itself, it turns out that since early times, humanity has believed in the idea of continuity after death – or reincarnation.

Today, too, there are hundreds of millions of people who believe that there is a definite reason why they were born, why they live in a particular place, and why certain things and not others happen to them. The notion of reincarnation makes the meaning of life on earth more profound.

What is the phenomenon of reincarnation? What does it mean?

Since the beginning of humankind, man has tried to deal with the phenomenon called death and define what we call the soul. During very ancient eras, the so-called "primitive" tribes would bury their dead dressed splendidly, adorned with jewels and equipped with implements and food in preparation for life after death.

Many philosophers, scientists, intellectuals and writers who left their mark on human culture based their philosophical theories on the idea of reincarnation. These include Plato, Pythagoras, Dante, Schopenhauer, Emerson, Nietzsche and Jung.

In 1989, an international survey was conducted in 12 European countries. About 25 percent of all Protestants and Catholics testified that they believe in the notion of rebirth. This is in spite of the fact that those religions do not officially accept the idea of and the belief in reincarnation.

In 1991, a survey that was conducted revealed that 58 million Americans believe in reincarnation.

This old-new notion constitutes the basis for the meaning of life on earth.

The people who lived on Earth in ancient times contemplated the forces of nature with amazement. They observed the sun and the other celestial bodies, the changing seasons, day and night, growth and corruption, ebb and tide, rain, hail, storms, lightning, earthquakes and volcanic eruptions. The terrifying forces of nature that controlled their lives became a topic of worship and religious ritual: the sun, the moon, water, fire, air and earth. Over the generations, while human beings developed and became increasingly aware, the mystery of birth and death continued to gnaw at their feeling of tranquillity. Like all the other creatures around them, human beings were involved in an unending struggle for survival, but they were different from the other creatures in that they *knew* that at the end of their lives, they would die and disappear.

The ancients devoted a great deal of time and resources to the subject of death. As long as fifty thousand years ago, human beings enjoyed holding stylized burial ceremonies. The tribal leaders were buried in their clothes, with various implements, food and flowers. The people who accompanied the deceased along his last path were guided by the concern for his soul. In the other world, on the other side – so they believed – he would have to hunt for food. That was humanity's first step in the direction of breaking away and separation from the world of the animals. They believed that the dead would come alive again, in one way or another, in the spirit world or in the physical world.

Ancient people believed that they had a soul that accompanied them throughout their lives. They linked the soul to breathing, which ceased at the moment of death. In Latin, the word *anima* (soul) means breathing.

One of their assumptions was that the soul was a kind of copy of the person, a passive part that accompanied him throughout his life. In their attempts to situate the soul, some people ruled that it resided in the aura that surrounds the human body. Others claimed that the soul accompanied the person like a shadow or a reflection, or, alternatively, resided in the genitals.

The notion of reincarnation was given a practical slant in a lecture given in Britain in the 1890s:

If a man feels that what, without any fault of his own, he suffers in this life can only be the result of some of his former acts, he will bear his sufferings with more resignation, like a debtor who is paying off an old debt. And if he knows besides that in this life he may actually lay by moral capital for the future, he has a motive for goodness, which is not more selfish than it ought to be. The belief that no act, whether good or bad, can be lost, is only the same belief in the moral world which our belief in the preservation of force is in the physical world. Nothing can be lost.

Max Müller, *Three Lectures on the Vedanta Philosophy* (1894)

The moment of death

There have been numerous attempts to explain what happens at the moment of death. The spark of life that disappears has been defined as a soul. Some people believed that the soul resembles a moth, butterfly or some other winged creature, which leaves the human body for the spirit world. The place through which the soul "leaves" the body is the mouth. This assumption was reinforced by what is known as "the sigh of death" that is so characteristic of human beings at the moment their lives end (they "breathe out their souls").

In many cultures, it was an accepted belief that the soul left the body in the form of a snake. In Australia, it was supposed that only the Shamans (medicine people) turned into snakes (the symbol of medicine!) when they died, while in other places it was thought that all human beings turn into snakes or worms.

Snakes of all types were identified with the soul and the death process. Lizards and reptiles in general were thought to be the gods of death that possessed great power. The snake also has a sexual connotation. This is because of its shape and its tendency to crawl and enter deep water or holes in the earth that are essentially similar to the female genitalia. In Africa, the snake served as a representative of the external soul and as the scion of the royal family. The snake constituted an inseparable part of certain ceremonies and rituals whose aim was to bless particular people. On the other hand, the death of the ritual snake also augured the certain death of the leader, and, as a result, the loss of the natural reproductive powers of the entire tribe. Such an event was a real crisis.

The soul in the form of a crawling snake

The ancients also identified the world of trees with the process of life and death. Trees were thought to be the center of the world because they had roots in the earth and branches that stretched toward the sky. In this way, they symbolized the bridge of the soul between what was above and what was below.

In Europe, there were prevalent beliefs that tightly linked the soul to the breath, the clouds in the sky or the birds. The Scots, for instance, believed in the necessity of leaving a window open in the dying person's room in order to facilitate the soul's exit. In other countries, it was believed that the soul becomes a cloud or a dove.

Ultimately, it was completely natural that such beliefs and customs throughout history led to the belief that after death, the soul is drawn into another body. This belief in fact constitutes the basis of reincarnation.

The Burmese belief is expressed in the following passage:

When a man dies his soul remains, his "I" has only changed its habitation. ... It is reborn among us, and it may even be recognized very often in its new abode. And that we should never forget this, that we should never doubt that this is true, it has been so ordered that many can remember something of these former lives of theirs. This belief is not to a Burman a mere theory, but is as true as anything he can see. For does he not daily see people who know of their former lives? Nay, does he not himself, often vaguely, have glimpses of that former life of his? No man seems to be quite without it, but of course it is clearer to some than others. Just as we tell stories in the dusk of ghosts and second sight, so do they, when the day's work is over, gossip of stories of second birth; only that they believe in them far more than we do in ghosts. ... Many children, the Burmese will tell you, remember their former lives. As they grow older the memories die away and they forget, but to the young children they are very clear. ...

This is the common belief of the people. ... A man has a soul, and it passes from life to life, as a traveller from inn to inn, till at length it is ended in heaven. But not till he has attained heaven in his heart will be attain heaven in reality.

H. Fielding Hall, *The Soul of a People* (1905)

Ancient Egypt

The ancient Egyptians believed in two aspects of awareness, called the "ka" (what attests to, a witness): the spiritual "ka" – the spiritual-holy witness, and the physical intermediary "ka" – the permanent witness. During a person's life, the "permanent witness" is contained in the person's bestial awareness. At the moment of death, it unites with the spiritual "ka" and attains liberation. After death, if the physical "ka" does not obey the spiritual "ka", a situation is liable to develop that forces it to undergo correction processes in other worlds, similar to those that occur on Earth.

As far as the ancient Egyptians were concerned, the physical "ka" had an ego and a constant hunger for the pleasures of this world, while the spiritual "ka" aspired to liberate itself from the moment of birth. In the Egyptian descriptions of life in the next world, the individual sought his eternal "ka" in order to achieve eternal life. A strong ego would attract a new body and create a new and fortified life, but, having said that, it would distance itself more and more from the guidance of the spiritual "ka". Such a phenomenon was liable to be expressed in a life that was conspicuous for its physical domination and hunger for power rather than spiritual achievements, sensitivity, and obedience to spiritual impulses. In such cases, there was a danger that the spiritual "ka" would retreat entirely and leave the awareness of the "I" to what is called "a second death", life in the animal, vegetable or mineral kingdom. This stage would continue until the soul happened to be given another opportunity.

The Egyptians based their entire culture on the belief in reincarnation. As a result, they created a powerful and important religion in their time. Moreover, this belief also contributed to the creation of a tremendous wealth of mystical and symbolic architecture as well as of works of art that reflected beliefs and tell us, to this day, about eternal gods. These gods "weigh" the soul after death. The power and beauty of the ancient Egyptian beliefs continue to fascinate us – even in the modern era in which we live.

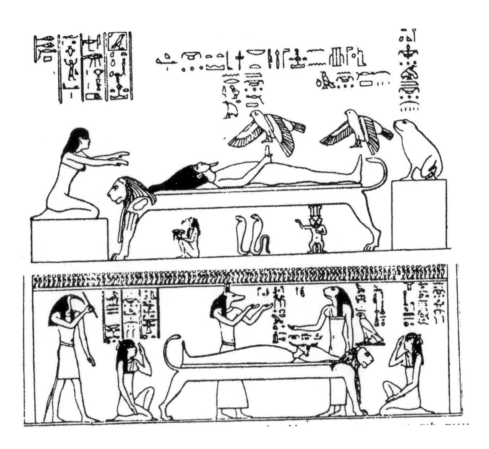

Isis praying to Horus beside the body of Osiris (above).
Anubis restores the body of Osiris to life (below).
Pictures from the rituals of the dead in Egypt.

In the myth of Osiris – the god of death – the belief in reincarnation received a great deal of support. Egyptian mythology contains a number of gods, among them Osiris, Isis, Horus and Set, who operated on different levels. The myth was actually anchored in the roots of an agricultural society that depended on the cyclical nature of the waters of the Nile that overflowed its banks and supplied the inhabitants of the earth with fertile soil; an astronomical myth that paralleled the location and movements of the stars, especially the annual rising of the star Syrius; a political myth that represented the relations between Upper Egypt and Lower Egypt, which were originally separate from each other; clear spiritual principles that originated in symbolism whose center was the reincarnation of the god.

The pharaonic cult employed a complex ritual in which every pharaoh was in fact an incarnation of Horus. His function was to observe the law, symbolized by the goddess Mat (or Maat). According to the belief, when one of the pharaohs left this world, he united with Osiris in the netherworld. His successor became a new incarnation – Horus' offspring and "relative" of Osiris and Isis. The myth, therefore, was dual. The dead pharaoh turns from Horus into Osiris, while simultaneously the heir to the throne turns into the son of Horus. It is easy to see how this process is parallel to birth, death and rebirth.

Osiris was the symbol and the one who made the Nile fertile, the earth was the body of Isis, while Horus was the atmosphere. Set had a dual symbolism. He was the enemy of Osiris, Isis and Horus. He was the dividing principle between time and intellect and therefore the one that destroyed life.

When the soul is reincarnated, death is the only possible result, after which rebirth occurs.

There are, according to Buddha's *Sangiti Sutta*, four modes of birth, each indicating the extent of awareness gained in previous lives:

Brethren, in this world, one comes into existence in the mother's womb without knowing, stays in it without knowing, and comes out from the mother's womb without knowing; this is the first.

Brethren, one comes into existence in the mother's womb knowingly, stays in it without knowing, and comes out from it without knowing; this is the second.

Brethren, one comes into existence in the mother's womb knowingly, stays in it knowingly, and comes out from it without knowing; this is the third.

Brethren, in this world, one comes into existence in the mother's womb knowingly, stays in it knowingly, and comes out from it knowingly; this is the fourth.

As quoted in W. Y. Evans-Wentz,
The Christian Doctrine of Rebirth (1921)

The Egyptian Book of the Dead

The Egyptian Book of the Dead is one of the most ancient books in existence in the world. It is a complex work that comprises over one hundred chapters. It seems that the information was transmitted orally over several generations prior to being written down. The book was written in hieroglyphics during the fifth dynasty and adorned with marvelous illustrations.

Like most Egyptian literature, the book was actually meant to be read by the kings. The book is a series of communications with the "ka" of the dead pharaoh, ascertaining his identification with Osiris and his journey into the netherworld in order to liberate himself or to be reborn. The message in the book is one of transformation: people are not what they are or what they can be. They have a divine spark in them and this spark must be the basis of their lives. The struggle of the gods can serve as a symbol of the inner struggle that exists in each of us during the course of our lives, especially when we are trying to live our lives according to the holy center – the soul – that is in us. The book is in fact a kind of guide for the "ka" and explains to the body-less souls the process that will make them eternal.

The psychological symbols of the Egyptian rituals bear a slight resemblance to those that appeared later in religions such as Hinduism, Buddhism and even Christianity. The events of our lives are weighed and judged in the moments after death. This judgment serves as a basis for the next life. Residues of the previous life pass into the next life as issues with which we have to deal.

This mythology places the cosmic process of reincarnation in a rich, broad and large perspective.

In Japan, Buddhist beliefs were expressed in the following way:

One particular attraction of Buddhist teaching was its simple and ingenious interpretation of nature. Countless matters which Shinto had never attempted to explain ... Buddhism expounded in detail. ... It explanations of the mysteries of birth, life, and death were at once consoling to pure minds, and wholesomely discomforting to bad consciences. It taught that the dead were happy or unhappy not directly because of the attention or the neglect shown them by the living, but because of their past conduct while in the body. ... To die was not to melt back into nature, but to be reincarnated. ...

A man ... was now sickly and poor, because in some previous existence he had been sensual and selfish. This woman was happy in her husband and her children, because in the time of a former birth she had proved herself a loving daughter and a faithful spouse; this other was wretched and childless, because in some anterior existence she had been a jealous wife and a cruel mother. ... The girl whom you hoped to marry has been refused you by her parents – given away to another. But once, in another existence, she was yours by promise; and you broke the pledge then given. Painful indeed the loss of your child; but his loss is the consequence of having, in some former life, refused affection where affection was due. Maimed by mishap, you can no longer earn your living as before. Yet this mishap is really due to the fact that in some previous existence you wantonly inflicted bodily injury.

Lafcadio Hearn, *Japan – An Attempt at Interpretation* (1904)

Maya and Sansara

Reincarnation constitutes a basic principle in the Buddhist religion and its philosophy.

Individual souls incarnate through worlds that are called *yogas*. Everything is created and then destroyed, only to be created once again. Life is a wheel on all levels. The creator, the god Vishnu, participates in the ongoing and repetitive process during which he himself dies and receives a new body. He incarnates and makes the world materialize again. In this creation, satanic forces whose main function is to oppose him also burst into the space of the world. They do everything in their power to dominate him and spoil the world he has created. Although this looks like a negative process, this struggle between opposing forces is in fact a natural process in the world.

The Brahmin/Atman are the components of universal awareness that are reflected by the goddess Maya.

The supreme goal of Hindu philosophy and religion is to penetrate the mystery of the universe and to guard the unity of the eternal spiritual world of the Atman. This world exists outside of the borders of time and beyond the borders of the visible. Jiotman is the final unit of awareness, and it belongs to the creatures that constitute the world, but thanks to a cosmic illusion, seems separated from Brahmin/Atman. Jiotman is parallel to what we call the soul.

The soul comes from the Brahmin/Atman, but is separated from it by the illusion of the goddess Maya. The Atman is immutable since it is located beyond time and space. The purpose of enlightenment (Muksha) is to rise above the ignorance (Abidia) that separates the Jiotman and the Atman. On the personal plane, the objective is to change the heart from a state of connection to the body and the physical world, above and beyond the lack of human perfection, to the coveted goal: rising above its physical action and existence.

The soul is eternal, but it carries with it the Jiveh – the illusion that it is separate from the Atman. This it how it was and this is how it will be, unless the soul achieves true enlightenment. Then it will get out of the cycle of birth, death and rebirth. There are souls that have always existed. They are sometimes born in the body of a man, and sometimes in the body of a woman. Every ego constitutes a psychological-physical unit that has a soul. This soul is not aware of the past and of its link to other souls. The ego is only a temporary expression of the Atman or the eternal soul.

The mythology and doctrine of Hinduism both express the view that the world began from the Atman, who was seeking salvation. The Kama is the Hindi god of love and, like Eros, the god of love in Greek mythology, was the first to be born to the gods after Chaos. He controls the domains of lust-will (kama-laka) and fulfills the principles of satisfaction. The people who forget the "self" remain tied to this dimension and are doomed to an eternal journey around the Samsara wheel. This is the wheel of time that turns between sexual intercourse, conception, birth, life, old age, and inevitably death.

After death, we go through various dimensions, starting from the spiritual, nebulous dimension, through a range of "paradises" and hell, until we reach the same dimension to which we are drawn and in which we are given an opportunity to fulfill our unrequited wishes – the ones we bring with us from our previous life. The process is slow, since we all prefer not to change, but rather to keep on fulfilling the same desires, whether we succeeded in doing so in the past or not.

For instance, a person who is compulsive in the realm of sex will not be satisfied with any number of sexual experiences, however numerous they may be. This is because his desire is located far beyond the fantasy or illusion of sexuality. Thus he is eternally trapped in the webs of Maya.

In India, people identify extensively with social castes. This rigid social position is also reflected in the idea of rebirth. The possibilities for mobility are small. The only path to freedom is the destruction of all the thoughts concerning the gods, all the thoughts or ideas of the Dharma (the path of justice). The loftiest characteristic is to live in a state of ongoing enlightenment.

There are people who believe that not all the souls incarnate to the same extent. Lofty and more developed creatures have the ability to incarnate more frequently. The purpose: to learn as many lessons as possible. Other souls incarnate less, if at all. They are completely unaware of the possibilities. This method produces spiritual goals that ultimately result in a perception that believes in the existence of many spheres and "paradises", each of which has its own complex hierarchy, laws and properties.

Because of the eternal continuity of the soul, birthdays are inconsequential in Tibet:

For the people the date of their King's birth [the Dalai Lama] is quite without interest. He represents in his person the return to earth of Chenrezi, the God of Grace, one of the thousand Living Buddhas who have renounced Nirvana in order to help mankind. ... With us it is generally, but mistakenly, believed that each rebirth takes place at the moment of the predecessor's death. This does not accord with Buddhist doctrine, which declares that years may pass before the god once more leaves the fields of Heaven and resumes the form of man.

Heinrich Harrer, *Seven Years in Tibet* (1954)

Discovering previous incarnations

Information concerning previous incarnations can come from any source: dreams, fantasies or even psychotherapy, Reiki and so on. The use of an astrological map is also one of the ways to clarify this kind of experience, as is the study of names and identities of people from the past by means of numerology.

Finding indisputable evidence of previous incarnations from the distant past is particularly difficult. This is because of the dearth of information regarding specific people, unless they held high positions, such as kings, queens, heroes or heroines.

In more advanced periods in which a larger amount of historical documentation exists, it is easier to prove and understand. However, we must remember that we all have periods in our lives that we favor more, since they arouse in us the desire for mystery and adventure. Certain times and periods spark our imagination more than others.

The thirteenth and final book of *The Desatir*, an ancient mystical work in the Mahabhadian language, was written by the prophet Zoroaster, and explains reincarnation:

Mezdam separated man from the other animals by the distinction of a soul, which is a free and independent substance, without a body or anything material, indivisible and without position, by which he attaineth to the glory of the Angels. ...

And everyone who wisheth to return to the lower world [the earth] and is a doer of good shall, according to his knowledge and conversation and actions, receive something, either as a King or a Prime Minister, or some high office or wealth, until he meeteth with a reward suited to his deeds. ... Those who, in the season of prosperity, experience pain and grief, suffer them on account of their words or deeds in a former body, for which the Most Just now punisheth them.

The Desatir, or *The Sacred Writings of the Ancient Persian Prophets*, translated by Mulla Firuz bin Kaus (1818)

soul mate and the law of karma

Many of us yearn to experience true love and meet our "soul mate" (or "twin soul"). A soul mate is someone who is familiar to us, a part of us, someone who makes us feel that we have always known him/her. Some people claim that they are unable to experience true happiness and complete love unless they find their soul mate.

When we meet somebody to whom we are powerfully attracted, we bring karma from previous lives into the relationship. In order to understand what is happening, it is important to compare the astrological map of the two people involved and find parallels. Such parallels are created when incarnations occur in parallel. The stars involved show us who we were in previous incarnations.

In Josephus Flavius' first-century book, *The Jewish War*, there is a description of the life and beliefs of the Essenes, who subscribed to the notion of reincarnation:

[The Essenes] condemn the miseries of life, and are above pain, by the generosity of their mind. And as for death ... our war with the Romans gave abundant evidence what great souls they had in their trails. ... They smiled in their very pains and laughed to scorn those who inflicted torments upon them, and resigned up their souls with great alacrity, as expecting to receive them again. For their doctrine is this, that bodies are corruptible, and that the matter they are made of is not permanent; but that the souls are immortal, and continue forever; and that they come out of the most subtile air, and are united to their bodies as to prisons, into which they are drawn by a certain natural enticement; but that when they are set free from the bonds of flesh, they then, as released from a long bondage, rejoice and mount upward. ... These are the divine doctrines of the Essenes about the soul, which lay an unavoidable bait for such as have once had a taste of their philosophy.

Josephus Flavius, *The Jewish War*

Rudolf Steiner and the laws of karma

Rudolf Steiner (1861-1925) is the principal researcher in the field of reincarnation in the 20th century. Steiner describes the action of the karma in reincarnation. In his opinion, there are chains of karmic links that endure from one incarnation to the next. There is a plan and a special rhythm in which we participate, and this is also what directs the flow toward certain people. By examining the time chart of the incarnations, we can investigate several examples of incarnations that are linked to one another.

The basic principle of reincarnation, according to Rudolf Steiner, is the Eastern idea of the Atman – "the man of power" – that is found in each one of us. Physical phenomena are only an expression of spiritual deeds. Beings that are revealed to our eyes in their physical form are the reflection of spiritual beings – the Atman.

In Steiner's opinion, reincarnation is a mechanism whereby it is possible to gain awareness that enables us to understand the laws of the entire universe.

Many other philosophers also supported Steiner's opinion: Goethe, Wagner, Emerson and Montague, despite the vigorous opposition on the part of Christian clerics on the one hand and scientists on the other.

Unlike in the East, Steiner did not believe in reincarnation that was characterized by the image of a wheel. He thought more in terms of a spiral that rises upward through stages of purification, beyond the earthly world. He found substantiation for his unconventional opinions in Jesus himself, who claimed that his spiritual brother, John the Baptist, had previously been the Prophet Elijah, the Jew.

The Hasidic play, *The Dybbuk*, explains reincarnation as understood by the Hasidim:

[If a man dies prematurely] what becomes of the life he has not lived...? What becomes of his joys and sorrows, and all the thoughts he had not time to think, and all the things he hadn't time to do...? No human life goes to waste. If one of us dies before his time, his soul returns to earth to complete its span, to do the things left undone and experience the happiness and griefs he would have known. ...

It's not only the poor it pays to be careful with. You can't say for a certainty, who any man might have been in his last existence, nor what he is doing on earth. ... Through many transmigrations, the human soul is drawn by pain and grief, as the child to its mother's breast, to the source of its being, the Exalted Throne above. But it sometimes happens that a soul which has attained to the final state of purification suddenly [through pride?] becomes the prey of evil forces which cause it to slip and fall. And the higher it has soared, the deeper it falls. ... [Such] vagrant souls which, finding neither rest nor harbor, pass into the bodies of the living, in the form of a Dybbuk, until they have attained purity. ...

The souls of the dead *do* return to earth, but not as disembodied spirits. Some must pass though many forms before they achieve purification.

S. Ansky, *The Dybbuk* (translation from 1926)

Personal experiences

In recent years, there has been a sharp increase in reports of all kinds of personal experiences people have had. Many have believed, written and heard stories and experiences – far more than can be proved scientifically.

Research in the field of reincarnation requires a combination of modern information and common sense. For instance, it is important to separate between the karmic history of the soul and the path it follows though the various incarnations on the one hand, and the personal character traits that are passed on from one generation to the next via heredity and biological laws – genetics – on the other. (However, it goes without saying that the following questions are asked: What is genetics? What is the memory contained in the DNA that is transferred from one generation to the next? What is genetic "waste" as it is called by scientist who, to this very day, are unable to provide an explanation for those specific genetic coils?) In reality, this kind of separation is not easy to implement.

Many people "remember" things in a collective memory that has accumulated over many generations. Not every such memory is necessarily a memory of a previous incarnation. We all have memories of which we are conscious and other memories in our subconscious. Memories from a previous life are also found in the subconscious, waiting for the appropriate time to surface to the plane of consciousness.

Many cases attest very convincingly to the existence of the phenomenon of reincarnation. Among others, one of the best-known cases was reported in Ian Cory's book, You Can't Die. This recounts the case of an Indian called Talingil who, a year before his death, promised that he would return to his niece as her son. He said that the child would bear the scars that he himself bore on his body as a result of an operation. Eighteen months later, the woman gave birth to a son. As promised, the scars were evident on his body. Thirteen months later, when the child was just beginning to talk, he burst out with the sentence: "Don't you know me? I'm Kahkodi" (the dead man's first name). Over the following years, the child identified various family members by name; he could describe places and provide information about events that had occurred prior to his birth. When he reached the age of nine, he began to "forget" events from his previous life, until his memories ceased completely at age 15.

The tenth-century Sufi master, Mansur Al-Hallaj, was a firm believer in reincarnation:

For a million years I floated in ether, even as the atom floats uncontrolled. If I do not actually remember that state of mine, I often dream of my atomic travels. I am but one soul but I have a hundred thousand bodies. Yet I am helpless, since Shariat (exoteric religion) holds my lips sealed. Two thousand men have I seen who were I; but none as good as I am now. ...

There have been thousands of changes in form. ... Look always to the form in the present; for, if you think of the forms in the past, you will separate yourself from your true Self. These are all states of the permanent which you have seen by dying. Why then do you turn your face from death? As the second stage has always been better than the first, then die happily and look forward to taking up a new and better form. Remember, and haste not. You must die before you improve. Like the sun, only when you set in the West can you rise again with brilliance in the East.

As quoted in Nadarbeg K. Mirza in *Reincarnation and Islam* (1927)

Going back in time by means of hypnosis

Going back in time by means of hypnosis is another important method of examining the phenomenon of reincarnation. The difficulty in this method is, of course, the need to investigate and validate the historical details that arise and are exposed during the process.

Clearly, not every woman who reports her experience of reincarnation was once Cleopatra. This is probably wishful thinking rather than reincarnation.

From the cases reported, it transpires that the average length of time that elapses between incarnations – that is, between death and rebirth – is about 52 years. It is often difficult to locate and examine documents that are over 75 years old, which makes things even more difficult for anyone who is interested in exploring these processes and phenomena.

The early Christian bishop of Hippo, Saint Augustine (354-430), initially examined the notion of reincarnation, but gradually rejected it:

[The Neoplatonist, Porphyry] was of opinion that human souls return indeed into human bodies [and not into animal bodies]. He shrank from the other opinion, lest a woman who had returned into a mule might possibly carry her own son on her back. He did not shrink, however, from a theory which admitted the possibility of a mother coming back into a girl and marrying her own son. How much more honorable a creed is that which was taught by the holy and truthful angels, uttered by the prophets who were moved by God's Spirit, preached by Him who was foretold as the coming Saviour by His forerunning heralds, and by the apostles whom He sent forth, and who filled the whole world with the gospel – how much more honorable, I say, is the belief that souls return once for all to their own bodies [at the resurrection], than that they return again and again to divers bodies?

Saint Augustine, *The City of God*

Reincarnation – second time round

After our initial survey, we will go back to what humanity has learned about reincarnation up until now.

What is the mysterious part of human beings that is supposed to be reborn after physical death, and why does it return?

Why do people generally not remember previous incarnations?

How is it possible to penetrate those subconscious memory banks?

What happens after death?

Why can't people incarnate as animals?

How can we explain the development of "the great teachers" of humanity via reincarnation?

Many scientists tend to reject all the theories concerning the continuation of life, claiming that they are nothing but worthless notions, similar to heartfelt wishes that will never come true. In this book, we will read about meticulously documented cases and about opinions and assessments from cultures that reinforce the claim that eternal life (in the form of reincarnation) actually exists. Perhaps that is the reason why an increasing number of people are taking an interest in the religions and philosophies of the Far East. Perhaps it is because of the promise of eternal life they contain.

However, it is important to stress that the notion of reincarnation is not exclusive to the Far East. All over the world, from the dawn of history, people have believed in eternal life – from Pythagoras and Plato up to the discussion between Dion Fortune and Rudolf Steiner in our day. The well-known psychologist, Carl Jung, Sigmund Freud's student, also believed in reincarnation.

The skeptics have always claimed that not a single person has returned from "the world beyond" in order to recount his/her experiences. However, the testimonies and stories of people who have undergone unexplained experiences are gradually mounting up, and the only way to understand them is by believing in reincarnation.

Whoever studies the history of ancient civilizations can find substantiation for the notion in ancient texts, legends and mythological stories.

We must remember that for hundreds of years, Western culture neglected the study of the question: Do human beings continue to live in one way or another after death?

For historical reasons, most of the philosophers and scholars of the 19th and 20th centuries espoused a materialistic and skeptical approach to human life, and totally rejected the mystical and philosophical approach that, in their opinion, was not practical. Awareness of "modern" ideas about the possibility of life after death occurred less than one hundred years ago!

Until recently, the puzzle of man in the university was approached from two different angles. The biologist Jacques Monod, author of *Opportunity and Need*, says: "Man was created in the universe completely by chance, unless we simplistically accept the theory of the Creation as it appears in religious sources. If not, we have to find natural explanations for it." As we know, the biblical notion of the creation constitutes a real problem for scientists. On the other hand, however, Monod also admits that the approach that holds that man was created totally by chance from raw material is a perception that is problematic in its own way. As in a gigantic puzzle, we are missing the one piece that would explain the existence of systems in the biosphere that operate as if there were coordination and purpose in their action. It is difficult to content ourselves with the simplistic definition of the beginning of life as "a chemical accident that has a poor chance of happening". Such an approach is no more realistic or logical than religious belief.

Scientists nowadays claim that "matter is everything". In contrast, people throughout the world today know that scientists have made, and still make, many mistakes, both in scientific research and in the use of science. There are ongoing and continuous arguments in the quest for different philosophies dealing with life after death. In various cultures, articles and books are published constantly, dealing with research on this field ranging from ancient ideas and religions to new theories concerning the existence of extraterrestrial beings in distant galaxies and so on.

We do not know what causes essential changes in people's views and beliefs, but there is no doubt that the period in which we are living is a time that is characterized by far-reaching changes. The question of the continuity of life is being examined once again.

Dr. Louis Thomas, a physician and scientist, wrote in his book, *The Life of the Cell*, that "death, in the general view, does not bother us." We can sit around the dinner table and talk about a war in which there are millions of casualties without becoming too upset. We can watch cases of sudden and shocking death on TV and in the cinema without batting an eyelid and without shedding a tear.

In many cases in which death is personal and close to us, we are gripped by shock. At the center of the problem lies the chilling fact of our death – our own. It is the only fact in nature whose existence we acknowledge with total certainty, but have difficulty talking or even thinking about.

Dr. Thomas was surprised when he found that seriously ill patients who were on the verge of death accepted death with equanimity and without fear. "Death is not bad, it's a natural process."

The question that has to be asked is as follows: Will we ever understand the meaning of the absence of consciousness? Where does awareness disappear to? Is it something that disappears and dissipates with the advent of death? Taking into account the fact that in nature, nothing gets lost or goes to waste, such a supposition does not seem natural.

Is there evidence of life after death?

Personal testimonies serve as a source for the study of the subject. Moreover, philosophers, scientists and researchers over the generations have devoted their time to examining it. They have thought about it and chosen the theory of rebirth in order to explain man's experience of eternity.

This book does not aim to convince people who do not believe. It invites those who are deliberating about the subject to expand their knowledge of the field, to study the opinions of the greatest philosophers, to read people's personal experiences, and to examine the various declarations and writings.

It seems that rebirth and reincarnation are intuitive feelings. We must remember that it is a matter of notions or knowledge that are common to different people in different cultures all over the world.

There are people who claim that reincarnation and rebirth are "romantic" notions, with no basis in reality.

Even if we ignore the fact that these ideas are supported by many scientists, anyone who reads "romantic poems" knows that life is bland without them. Do the romantic poets and writers not express "truth" – their own view of life? And even if it is not the whole truth, this does not detract from the importance of their contribution. No wise person will expect a single idea or approach to contain all of the truths. In matters such as these, the reader has to contribute something of his own.

The historian, A. T. Bacall, who lived in the 19th century, said: "If eternal life is not truth, there is very little importance to anything else – whether it is true or not."

A century later, Edmund Wilson said: "The knowledge that death is not so far away, that my mind and my feelings, like my vitality, will disappear as quickly as a smoke ring, has one effect on earthly matters. Everything becomes less important… It is difficult to take life seriously, including personal endeavors and achievements."

W. McNeill Dixon, who wrote *The Human Condition*, is considered to be "the Confucius of the West". The *New York Times* has selected his books as being among the most important works of the twentieth century. According to Dixon, the history of mankind is a long story filled with suffering. For those who have suffered a cruel fate, there is neither explanation nor consolation. These wretched souls, who are intellectually and morally confused, entered their lives and existence as if they were blind, and will leave them in the same way. They are not aware of their origin, of the meaning of their lives, or of the reason that their lives, which are "above lowly creatures", are full of misery and agony.

According to the accepted way of thinking, living means walking nowhere along a difficult path. How can a path that leads nowhere have any meaning?

Life that contains suffering and pain, that ends arbitrarily in the same way as it began, is an absurd idea. According to this approach, there is nothing to be hoped for, to look forward to, and there is nothing that can be done, until we are destroyed.

The words "eternal life" are words that express everything that is most special and dear to us – the soul. When it goes, nothing worth keeping is left in this world. At the moment of death, something entirely different happens. The sky is illuminated with a intense light, the door opens to innumerable possibilities…

What kind of eternal life can be grasped by human awareness?

Of all the existing philosophical approaches, the claim regarding rebirth and reincarnation is the oldest and most accepted.

We all think in terms of the future. All human ideas are linked to the future to the point that when certain people manifest a lack of faith in the concept that man is an eternal being, it casts doubt upon the entire future. And then the question of how they could ever have been born is asked.

Deep inside ourselves, we are secretly aware of our part in the "eternal spring of creation", in the hope that, some time in the future, we can return and find life in it.

If things as they are today have nothing in common with things as they will be, it means that we do not have any basis according to which we can even relate to the future. Human beings cannot think about and relate to their existence without the concept of "time". Any approach that insists upon existence in the present only, and refutes spiritual life as a possible continuation of the present, actually transforms the present into a completely insoluble and incomprehensible problem.

The philosopher Plato believed that our present knowledge is in fact a collection of what was learned or what our soul knew in a previous state or life.

However, there are people who claim that we do not remember anything about our previous lives. (This is the place to mention that even in everyday life, we don't remember the events that occur in our lives on a daily basis accurately, from the day they began.) "Lost memories", as psychologists and scientists explain to us, are important findings that can be reconstructed. Nothing gets lost. Experiences of the past contribute to our life experience and our ability, and serve as a contribution to all layers of the personality.

It is possible that this is exactly the situation with regard to previous lives, when each incarnation constitutes one day in a long series of human history.

According to Plato, the soul is liberated at the moment of death from the dimensions of time and space, and returns to its source. After a certain period of quiet and solitude, it returns to incarnate in a human body.

For purposes of the present discussion, it is not important what the exact nature of the soul is – it never separates from the "self". It is the center of everything, and without it there is neither awareness nor thought. It is impossible to separate the self from the atom, from emptiness, from space and time. The philosophers of the future will think in a new way, different than what was accepted in the past. They will accord the "self" special status, which will also be appropriate.

It may well be that man is a much more interesting and important being than we have thought up until now, a being with supreme cosmic importance.

As stated previously, many scientists refute theories of eternal life, claiming that the latter belong to the type of sweet illusions nurtured by incurable romantics. Obviously, if the belief in eternal life is based on the individual and personal desire of some person or other to come back to life, it does not make the theory into a reality. In contrast, if a person who suffered in his life complains that he has to come back to life in another incarnation, this claim does not mean that reincarnation does not exist. On the contrary, it is possible that the second person is angry that in this life he is paying for things he did in his previous lives, and that in the next life he will pay an even heavier price for his misdeeds in this life.

Dr. J. Paul Williams served as head of the department of medicine at Mount Holyoak College in the United States. His opinions were anchored in the fields of religion, philosophy and science.

He based his opinions on the belief that prevails in the East, among the followers of the great religions – Buddhism and Hinduism – which state that eternal life is certainly a fact. They believe that people are born over and over again in order to live in this world, and this process is accompanied by great anxiety. The reasons for this are complex, and the followers of these religions learn how it is possible to avoid being born again. They do not want it, and perceive another incarnation as a punishment. The coveted goal for a Hindu or Buddhist believer is to find a way out of the "circle of life".

The claim that the human being is a soul allows the assumption – which is not illogical – that the soul can survive physical death. If a person is only a body, a psycho-chemical reaction and no more, there is no doubt that he will not come back and live again in a physical form. As stated above, if a person is a soul, the possibility remains open for the soul to remain after physical death.

Is the person a body that has a soul or a soul that found a body in which to reside?

There are two accepted ways to prove each theory. One is to show a logical sequence of events from a series of correct hypotheses. The second is simply to point and say: "That's how it is!"

Many people believe in the existence of the soul on an emotional level, from experience in life and personal experience. However, such feelings do not constitute scientific proof.

The belief that people are only physical bodies is just one of a set of beliefs that state that only "matter exists". The "spirit" does not exist at all. There are respected scientists who have expanded and consolidated this hypothesis. Many people believe in these scientists and their opinions. In contrast, there are just as many equally competent scientists who do not believe that this universe is made of "matter" only. They espouse the approach that belief in eternal life is possible – in other words, it is not simply romantic nonsense. This is mainly a philosophical question and all of us, when we examine it, have to be philosophers to a certain extent.

Even if you believe that we, as human beings, are souls, you have not yet proved the existence of eternal life. Do the souls survive physical death? Our only experience as living human beings is through our link with our bodies.

There are people who claim that from this simple fact, we have to draw the conclusion that if we do not have a body, we do not have life. However, this is not an obligatory conclusion. William James claimed that two approaches can exist with regard to the relation between the body and life. One states that the body creates life. The second states that the body reflects life, just as light is produced by the candle, but the candle does not stop existing if the light is extinguished. The moment the candle goes out, the flame disappears. The flame can be reflected in a mirror. If the mirror is moved, the light will continue to exist.

Can we accept the hypothesis that the body reflects life with the same ease as we accept the more widespread hypothesis that the body "produces" the soul?

Can a human body, which consists solely of pain and suffering and lacks a soul, create works such as *Hamlet* (Shakespeare), the theory of evolution (Darwin) or the theory of psychoanalysis (Freud)? It is easier to assume, even on the basis of these few examples, that these brilliant achievements were produced by souls that used the human body as a "tool" for realization on earth.

If we accept the hypothesis that the soul is reflected in the body, and is not "produced" by it, we can easily and logically assume and believe that the soul can exist separately from the physical body.

The weak link in this argument is, of course, the unsolved problem of the lack of our "direct connection" with the soul , but this does not mean that it is not possible.

We can claim that it is not possible to "experience" the existence of atoms and electrons directly either, which does not negate the truth. We believe in it because we have indisputable "proof" of it. However, we do not accuse the scientists of unrealistic hypotheses when they try to tell us that a rock made of solid stone is actually a combination of atoms, electrons and protons that move at a high speed.

Another layer that reinforces the possibility of eternal life is very simple: We live now. As human beings, we cannot understand the limits of time. If this is true, our chances of existing are non-existent. However, in any case, against all odds – we're here. The only way to settle this contradiction is to assume that we – like time itself – are infinite.

A human being emerges close to the time of his birth. He lives, and ultimately he dies. In his death, he becomes eternal.

If a person believes in eternal life and in incarnations, he has to believe that he will live after his present death as well, as he lived previously, before he was born the last time.

There are reasons that cause us to forget our previous incarnations, and anyone who believes in eternal life also believes that certain means were adopted to this end.

One of the basic hypotheses of modern science states that existence is stable, observes certain laws, and is certainly not subject to "whims".

After the death of his wife, George Herbert Palmer wrote: "Feelings of sorrow and remorse will not be found to be suitable following her death, but how is it possible to call the world a rational place if a collection of particles of matter created such a comely soul?"

The philosopher C. J. Dukes, president of the American Philosophers' Association, head of the philosophy department at Brown University for 30 years, was interested in a range of fields – art, science and languages – and wrote about them.

In two of his books, he touches on certain aspects that are linked to reincarnation: *A Critical Analysis of the Belief in Life after Death* and *Awareness and Death*. His 1960 work that bears the title *Life after Death – Reincarnation* is devoted entirely to this subject.

In his opinion, there is a certain "order" according to which there is life after the death of the physical body. This belief is widespread because of its source and its nature, which is similar to a large extent to the belief in the existence of God.

Professor J. B. Pratt once said: "We begin to believe in God because they tell us that this is how it is. However, the belief in the continuity of life has a spontaneous source. A child who is aware of his present existence accepts the basic assumption of the continuity of life as an obvious and natural thing. In fact, death is something new that must be learned, from the child's point of view."

According to Dukes, the members of the Jewish and Christian religions want to believe in reincarnation despite the fact that the belief in death is actually more paradoxical.

The cleric, W. R. Alger, wrote: "No subject had such an effect on humankind as the possibility that when the soul leaves the body, it is reborn in another body, according to its character, the surroundings and its deeds." Although this idea (karma) is different than the idea of rebirth, both of them dovetail from the logical point of view.

The idea explains in a wonderfully detailed and coordinated manner the chaos, the iniquitous lack of justice, the evil and the suffering that are evident in people's lives. Anyone who can accept this theory will find great relief in the immediate comprehension of the injustice in the world. This belief explains all the phenomena from which the fabric of human life is woven. When we observe life from a belief in karma and rebirth, we see the world in a way in which the material and spiritual elements become united with the entire ordered system that operates according to predetermined laws. Human existence becomes a whole picture of perfect poetic justice.

Survival in the sense of rebirth immediately evokes the question of whether our present life is not one of those incarnations, some of which we have already been through. However, this being the case, a tremendous objection arises in us, based on the question: Why do we not remember anything about our previous lives?

If we assume that a lack of memory attests and "proves" that if there is no memory, there is no life, there will be far-reaching consequences. It can prove, for instance, that we did not exist during the first years of our lives in our present body. Furthermore, people do sometimes evoke memories and testimonies that are linked to previous lives.

One of the best-known cases in the literature is that of "the rebirth of Katsuguru", which was studied scientifically and beyond any shadow of a doubt. This case was documented by Lefsidio Eren.

It tells of a small child called Katsuguru, the son of a man called Ganzu, in a village called Nakanumura. The child declared that in a previous life, he had been called Tozo. He was the son of a farmer called Kyobai, and his mother was a woman calld Shiduzo. According to him, the family lived in a village called Kodokubu. The father died, and a man called Hanshiru took his place. Tozo himself died of smallpox at age six, a year after his father's death.

He described the funeral, gave a precise account of his previous parents and of the house in which he lived. Ultimately, the child was taken to the village, where he showed the adults the way, and identified the people, who confirmed the facts he described. Later, he pointed at a store and a tree, and declared that they had not been there before.

Testimonies of this kind are very important to the question of rebirth. The knowledge of such details, as seen in the above-mentioned case, is too detailed and circumstantial for it to be coincidental. It is not a case of *déjà vu* that is fully understood and explained by psychologists. Indeed, while this kind of testimony does not serve as incontrovertible proof of the idea of rebirth, there is not doubt that it cannot be discounted outright.

Another objection to the idea of rebirth stems from the claim that if there is no awareness and identity, as "provided by the memory", rebirth actually has no meaning. There is no difference between a person's death and rebirth and final, total death, if we do not have any way of remembering what happened.

In this context, we will quote Leibniz: "What point is there in the fact that God will turn you, sir, into the king of China, if you don't remember what you were previously? Will it not be the same thing if God had destroyed you, and recreated the king of China?"

The important point is not the memories themselves, but rather the awareness of the ongoing memory. None of us is particularly disturbed by the lack of early childhood memories. The feeling of identity depends on the gradual nature of change that occurs in us, of which we are not aware all the time. The feeling of passing time astounds us sometimes, when we suddenly become aware that too much time has elapsed for us to learn anything by looking at old pictures or letters from decades ago. Such letters and pictures will not help us remember important details, such as who the letter was for and what it was about. The person who wrote the letter is not the same person who is reading the letter today, in all possible senses.

There are people who claim that without previous memories, we do not know what we are being "rewarded" or "punished" for in this life. Without memory, we cannot learn anything, and the lesson is wasted. However, the theory of punishment in the style of "an eye for an eye" and "a tooth for a tooth" is not the only one, nor, of course is it the most effective one.

For instance: Two people quarrel, and during the course of the argument, a skirmish ensues. The first person injures the second one. The law of karma will cause the first person to receive a lesson in forbearance and tolerance, and will not necessarily cause him to be injured in exactly the same way by the second person... Or perhaps he will suffer from a disappointment in love that will force him to wait for his beloved year after year...

Many of us, upon reaching maturity, can discern "automatic" patterns in our lives that dictated the course of our lives, like a guiding hand from above. Changes that occur in the social realm, work, among friends, as well as internal changes, cause us to be what we are.

These phenomena that happen to us during our lives can happen in the most natural way between one period of life and the next.

The American minister and scholar, William R. Alger (1822-1905), expressed his views about reincarnation:

The argument [for reincarnation] from analogy is especially strong. It is natural to argue from the universal spectacle of incarnated life that this is the eternal scheme everywhere, the variety of souls finding in the variety of worlds an everlasting series of adventures in appropriate organisms.

It must be confessed that of all the thoughtful and refined forms of the belief in a future life none has had so extensive and prolonged prevalence as this. It has the vote of the majority, having for ages on ages been held by half the human race with an intensity of conviction almost without a parallel. Indeed, the most striking fact at first sight about the doctrine of the repeated incarnations of the soul ... is the constant reappearance of the faith in all parts of the world, and its permanent hold on certain great nations.

As quoted in E. D. Walker, *Reincarnation, A Study of Forgotten Truth* (1878)

Karma, rebirth, free will

In 1958, Dr. Smith Huston published a book entitled *Man's Religion*. In this book, the dialogue between the cultures of the East and the West is reinforced. Smith Huston was born in China to parents of American origin, and when he grew up, he served for many years as a professor of philosophy at MIT, and also taught religion at the University of Syracuse. In his book, he discusses reincarnation in relation to the law of karma. Although karma is defined as a moral law that is based on cause and effect, there are many people who consider it to be a kind of cosmic bookkeeping.

The author proposes that we see karma in a slightly different light: cosmic harmony. When this harmony is upset for some reason or other, it has to be adjusted. Members of Western cultures tend to view karma as a punishment. In contrast, people in the East relate to the same notion positively. Buddha claims that karma's "heart is made of love, its end is peace and quiet, and its course is sweet".

This could mean that our deeds teach us how, ultimately, to bring greater harmony into our lives. Everything depends on our "talent" and desire to make an effort.

The scientific world warns us over and over again about the importance of the principle of cause and effect in the physical world. This principle can be applied in all fields of life: environmental pollution, massive exploitation of natural resources, destruction of the rainforests, and, on the personal level, leading a lifestyle of one kind or another.

Every action in life has a result. Proverbs such as "You will reap what you sow" are examples of this principle. We can also say: "Sow a thought and you will reap a deed, sow a deed and you will reap a habit, sow a habit and you will reap character, sow character and you will reap fate."

In the East, the law of cause and effect is tighter, obligating, and brooks no irregularities. The present condition of every person – how happy, tranquil or confused he is, to what extent he can see – depends on what he wanted and achieved in his past; and in parallel, his thoughts and decisions in the present define his future.

Members of the Hindu religion understand the notion of karma as a perfect value-oriented law that directs the universe and obliges every person in a personal manner. However, most of the people refuse to acknowledge this. They prefer to "transfer" the source of their problems outward, away from themselves. Such an approach, according to Hinduism, is simply immature.

Since karma claims to be like the universe, which operates according to clear laws, it is often interpreted as fatalism. This is incorrect. According to karma, every decision has a consequence, but decision-making is a path down which people walk freely and have the possibility of choosing.

From another point of view, we can say that the consequences of a person's actions in his past determine his life in the present.

Exactly like a card player finds himself in a given situation with certain cards, but still has the possibility of choosing how he will play, a soul that passes from life to life in innumerable human bodies is in fact guided by its decisions.

According to the Hindu religion, the soul does not depend on the physical body more than the body depends on the clothes it wears or the house in which it lives. When the clothing gets old or becomes too small, we replace it. This is what the souls do, too. In order to reach this level of awareness, we have to examine how we express ourselves. The word "my" separates the object whose ownership we are declaring from us. When we speak about our house, it does not mean that we think that we are the house. We talk about our bodies, our opinions, our personalities in that way. That way of speaking attests to the fact that in a certain sense, we tend to think of ourselves as separate from those parts.

What is the "I" that includes in it my body and soul, but is not identified with them?

Science maintains that our (physical) body does not contain a single thing that was with us seven years ago. During our lives, our personalities and opinions change in a basic manner. However, in spite of all the changes, something remains. The same "something" is deeper than the body or the personality, and provides the nucleus for continuity within the occurrence of the change.

The word "personality" comes from the Latin word *persona*, which originally meant a mask with which the actor covers his face when he goes on to the stage. The role of the mask is to serve as a substitute for makeup, which characterizes the character and the role, while the actor behind the mask remains anonymous and hidden.

The mask is our personality, the role to which we are born and chosen during the greatest drama – life.

Of course, the problem occurs as a result of the fact that most of us forget the difference between the role and the real "I". The personality is simply "the present clothing" that will be discarded when the present play ends. We are drawn into the present outlines of life and cannot remember our previous roles or plan what will happen in the future. The aim is to correct the mistaken identities. When a person succeeds in turning his awareness inward, he penetrates all the "masks" and ultimately reaches the anonymous actor who is situated deep inside.

"In all of his journeys, the person is not alone – from the beginning to the end he is deeply entrenched – the Atman – the point of light, the self, the infinite, the smallest part that can no longer be divided."

The German theologian, Richard Wilhelm (1873-1930), wrote an article called "Reincarnation" in which he said the following:

Let us consider what attitude to take toward this idea. In the first place we must insist that, from the viewpoint of Christianity, it is absolutely feasible. Christianity, it is true, lays stress only on the law of Karma, though it remains silent as to the working of its operations; looking only to its ultimate consummation, it does not touch upon the intervening stages. ...

Unprejudiced observation and reasonable reflection lead us to the conviction that this law [of Karma actually exists. However, in one life, bounded by birth and death, we can only experience a part of the whole of existence. We live through certain occurrences in which one tangled skein of Karmic effects is unraveled, while at the same time new threads of Karma are spun that cannot be worked out in this life, because their disentanglement is cut short by death. On the other hand we see results come to fruition, the causes of which are not to be found in this life. These are the great problems with which a Job battles, and to which – in spite of all faith in a hereafter – only the words "and yet?" of the Psalmist must be uttered, if the Wisdom of the East is not called to our aid. And so it is easy to understand that many of our deepest and clearest thinkers, as for instance Lessing and Goethe, look upon reincarnation as a theory well worthy of consideration.

Richard Wilhelm, in *The Theosophical Path* (January 1924)

Fragments of the lost whole –
reincarnation and mythologies

The cycle of birth, life, death and rebirth is the basic topic of Alan West's work on myths and religion: *The Wisdom of the Serpent – The Mythology of Death, Rebirth and Reincarnation.*

According to West, there is nothing more provocative than the notion of death. Knowledge of death is the reason why man created the sciences, the arts, religion and philosophy.

Difficult human questions that pose an interesting challenge include: How would it feel to go to sleep and not wake up? Where was I a moment prior to fertilization (when sperm and ovum united)? The thought about what happens before death is as impossible as the thought about what happens after death. If I came from "nothing", there is every chance that I will return to the same "nothing" once again.

In the 19th century, scholars reached the conclusion that mythological stories were a phenomenon that had developed since the dawn of humanity. In their opinion, these stories did not have any basis in truth other than primitive man's observation of the world around him, of the heavenly bodies, of nature and the phenomena that he was unable to explain.

Today, there are more developed theories as to the source of the various mythological stories. In the well-known essay by Irwin Thomson, *"On the Threshold of History"*, the author writes that mythology is not an early stage in human development, but rather a description of reality in which the known is mingled with the unknown via a method that combines spirit and matter, I, society, universe – all expressed in an esoteric language of poetry and numbers.

In his book about mythologies, Giorgio di Santilena speaks about a broad global structure of thoughts that existed prior to the time of the ancient Greeks, and has endured to this day in the form of mythological stories and fairy-tales, which are not understood today as they were supposed to be. The people who were considered to be among the few who succeeded in preserving fragments of the "lost whole" were Plato, who gave the West the basis of modern philosophy, and Pythagoras.

Bruno Bettelheim, who enjoys a worldwide reputation in child psychology, writes about "the meaning and importance of legends" in *The Uses of Magic*: "In most of the cultures, there is no significant difference between mythology, folk-tales and children's legends. In Nordic countries, there is one collective word for these kinds of literature: saga. Some of the legends and the popular stories stem from mythological stories and others are combined in one another. They all describe society's experiences and ancient wisdom that passes from one generation to the next. Mythology transfers its topics in a unique way, larger than life, with spiritual power. The lofty and sacred divine power is presented by superhuman heroes who are in a state of interaction with human beings. Children's legends are presented in a simpler manner. The listener or reader is not required to make any kind of effort. Stories of this type encourage, give hope for the future, and allow a happy ending."

The Russian Christian philosopher, Nicolas Berdyaev (1874-1948), grappled with the problem of reincarnation in theology:

The popularity of Theosophy and Anthroposophy is due precisely to the teaching of reincarnation. And the weakness and unreasonableness of theologic teachings concerning the genesis of the soul and its final destiny are responsible for this popularity. It is difficult to reconcile oneself to the traditional teaching according to which the soul is created at the moment of conception and at this moment the primordial sin is communicated as if it were a communicable disease. Also it is difficult to accept the other teaching, according to which the soul is a product of a hereditary process and receives the primordial sin as it would receive an hereditary disease. Neither of these teachings ... supply any justification whatsoever for human sufferings and the injustices of individual destiny. But most intolerable is the teaching of eternal suffering in Hell. ... Any attempt to construct a sensible teaching about Hell awakens moral protest. ...

The teaching of reincarnation is simple. It makes rational the mystery of human destiny and ... reconciles man to the [apparent] unjust and incomprehensible sufferings of life ... man stops comparing his destiny with the happier destiny of other people and accepts it.

Nicolas Berdyaev, in *Transmigration of Souls* (n.d.)

The phoenix – the symbol of eternity

For thousands of years, the main symbol of eternity and rebirth has been the phoenix, a unique and beautiful legendary bird that lives for a long time (500-600 years) and inhabits the wilderness. The legend states that ultimately, the bird burns up only to emerge young and fresh from the ashes and live through another incarnation of hundreds of years. When it is consumed by the flames, a single spark, which symbolizes its eternal part, is supposed to remain. The new life develops from it.

A similar legend exists in the *Phybeologos* – a collection of about fifty Christian allegories that relate to the animal world. Although this literary material was banned by the church, it was read enthusiastically during the Middle Ages. The phoenix is described there as a wondrous creature that originated in India, floating on the wings of the winds for 500 years. Afterwards, following the aroma of spices, it flies to Egypt, where it enters the temple of Heliopolis. The bird burns on the altar until it becomes ashes. The next day, the young and new bird rises from the ashes already covered with feathers. On the third day, the bird salutes the priest and flies off.

E. V. Conley, a writer who lived in the 19th century, mentioned that it is a particularly interesting phenomenon to find similar mythological stories among different peoples that lived so far away from one another. The phoenix also appears in ancient legends from Ireland, Japan (where it is called Kirin), and Turkey (where it is called Karkas).

Of course, the central idea in the phoenix allegory suggests the notion of eternal life and rebirth, but it has many aspects in the sense of the life of the soul, history and age. Even the idea that this bird is one of a kind, and therefore does not have a mate, is significant: the being that undergoes reincarnation is sexless and spiritual.

According to Conley, the phoenix represents the construction and destruction of the world, which, in the opinion of many, is caused by fire.

Herodotus also mentioned the phoenix, and described it as a legendary and sacred bird. The bird is frequently mentioned in the Egyptian *"Book of the Dead"*, where it is called "the bird of Hebnu. It is surmised that the source of the legend of the bird lies in Greece, where it symbolized the spirit and the soul that are never-ending.

Ultimately, the highest level following death is reached. The Egyptian Book of the Dead states: "I am the bird of Hebnu, the heart and soul of Ra… the heart and soul of the gods, or enlightened beings, that come down every now and then to the earth according to their wish. The soul-spirit undergoes a special process. It is destroyed and is then rebuilt in a new form, with every layer of its physical form loftier than the previous one."

The philosopher, P. M. Cornford, from Cambridge University, wrote in his book *From Religion to Philosophy*: "Reincarnation is a basic doctrine in the field of mysticism. This life, which renews itself ceaselessly, is created from the opposite condition which is called death. On the other side of the spectrum, it finishes once again. In this idea of reincarnation we find the first understanding of the circle of existence, the circle of life, which divides into two parts – darkness and light. Life, or the soul, goes on an endless journey from one side to the other, imprisoned in the wheel of time, preserving its personal identity. The soul passes through all forms of life, and is not actually 'human'. Human life is nothing but one form of many through which the soul passes. The soul is sacred and eternal, and is made of the same substance that all the souls in the world are made of. In this sense, the unity of life is preserved. However, on the other hand, every soul has its atomic uniqueness that is preserved throughout all the incarnations."

In the art and architecture of the Buddhist culture, the wheel of life is described as a symbol of karma and rebirth. This symbol also appears on the Buddhist flag. Immediately after Buddha attained enlightenment, his first ceremony was called "turning the wheel of the law". The wheel of rebirth is also found in Greece and Italy, as well as in Crete, in works attributed to the fourth and fifth centuries BCE. Also, see the Tarot cards.

From a philosophical point of view, it is also possible to view the wheel of life as a powerful symbol of the human struggle for enlightenment and harmony – identification and development of the awareness, the body and the personality. All these lead to an unbalanced outlook. The quiet center of the wheel of life – where the "eternal I" is located – is the highest place that can be reached. The ups and downs of rebirth, even when one experiences them, will not cause a feeling of loss or spiritual suffering. As Krishna says in the Bashvad-Ghita: "In the heart of every creature there is the Master – Yeshvara – who, by dint of his magic causes all things and creatures to move on the universal wheel of time, to find in it a shelter for your soul." Yeshvara is the essence, the sexless spirit that is found in every creature in creation.

Joseph Campbell said: "Those that identify themselves with the human body they have been given cannot avoid unnecessary pain and suffering, because for them the end of the body is the end of everything."

Conversely, those who have found the quiet point of eternity inside them, around which everything moves, accept all things as they are. In the perception of the West with regard to the figure of "the hero", he claims, the hero is in fact a certain person, a human, whose end is death.

In the East, in contrast, the hero is a mythological figure that undergoes incarnations. As is quoted from the Ghita: "He is never born, he never dies, he never was, and he never will be. He is eternal, he does not change, and he is very old."

Albert Schweitzer (1875-1965), who was a physician, a clergyman and a musician, explained the notion of reincarnation in the following way:

The idea of reincarnation contains a most comforting explanation of reality by means of which Indian thought surmounts difficulties which baffle the thinkers of Europe. ... By reason of the idea of reincarnation Indian thought can be reconciled to the fact that so many people in their minds and actions are still so engrossed in the world. If we assume that we have but one existence, there arises the insoluble problem of what becomes of the spiritual ego which has lost all contact with the Eternal. Those who hold the doctrine of reincarnation are faced by no such problem. For them that non-spiritual attitude only means that those men and women have not yet attained to the purified form of existence in which they are capable of knowing the truth and translating it into action.

Albert Schweitzer,
Indian Thought and Its Development (1952)

A flood in Bangladesh

Jan packed his things and climbed onto the plane, with no intention of returning. He felt as if he had never left Bangladesh.

During the previous year, he had not stopped dreaming about black-skinned, sharp-featured children and people swimming in the turbulent water, sailing simple wooden boats, fishing or standing in the endless rice paddies.

When he spoke about dreams with his friend from the university, psychiatrist and professor van Riebeeck, the latter suggested that he undergo a process of hypnosis. Initially, Jan demurred, but finally curiosity won the day. He met with van Riebeeck five times in all. During the course of their meetings, it became clear to him that he had lived in Bangladesh in the past. What he had seen in his dreams were authentic pictures from the life of the natives. He saw himself as a small boy, black-skinned, drowning with his parents and sister in a big flood, one of many that occur in the region each year.

Jan, 53 years old, was born in a small neighborhood in Amsterdam, Holland, and grew up there. A thin, light-skinned child with pale eyes and yellow hair, he was the third of seven children born to his impoverished parents.

When they all played, he was the only one who helped his two older sisters with the housework. At a very young age, he decided that he would study at the university and acquire a steady profession. When he was 10, he approached a small bakery near his house, and raced through the streets of the neighborhood on his bicycle in the mornings, delivering fresh rolls and milk. He gave the money to his parents. In high school, the exceptional talent and ambition of the tall, skinny youth did not go unnoticed, and he was awarded a generous scholarship. That paved his way to the university. Jan spent seven long years studying engineering and specializing in dams. He completed his studies *cum laude*. For over 20 years, he worked and helped all the members of his family. He never married or established a home. Somehow, he did not feel that he belonged. Until the dreams started...

At the end of that year, his parents were killed in a road accident. Jan felt isolated and at a loose end. His siblings, who had married, had scattered all over the country. For his part, he felt that he wanted to travel to some distant place - to the place that appeared every night in his dreams.

In 1988, the Bramahputra River overflowed its banks. In certain places, the torrents of water reached a radius of over 10 miles. The high stone dikes collapsed like grains of gravel. The enormous amounts of water that flowed down from the Himalayan Mountains caused tens of thousands of people to drown as they were swept away by the rush of water. The capital, Dakka, was damaged, but remained standing.

The only white man to die in the flood, as was written in the newspaper, was Jan van Riebeeck - the dam expert.

In a lecture, Arthur P. Shepherd (1885-1968), the Canon of Worcester Cathedral, England, relates to the idea of reincarnation as follows:

If we take into our unprejudiced thinking the picture of reincarnation as the process of human evolution, we shall find in it the answer to the problems of the new world situation. ... So too, the vast picture of the meaningless masses and movements of the [starry] nebulae resolves itself into a universe of spirit beings, in infinite creative relationships to one another and to man. The perplexity of history, with its procession of rising and falling civilizations, is seen as mankind's pilgrimage of spiritual descent and ascent, in which we have all taken part, and in which recurring individual reincarnation is the principle of unification and progress. So too, the apparent inadequacy of a single earth life, or its bondage to physical or mental or moral or circumstantial deficiency, is given new hope and understanding in the realization of the process of reincarnation. Finally, there is the certainty that in all this man has never been alone. The Christ, whose earthly incarnation the Gospels declare to us, has always shepherded man's path of evolution, and since His descent into our earthly life He is always with us, to be found by those who seek Him.

Arthur P. Shepherd (1961)

From Ireland with love

Edith Pior lived her entire life in New York. She was widowed at age 22 after only one year of marriage. She was young and beautiful and knew that the future lay ahead. Two years later, she married Bruce Goldwyn, a pharmacist by profession, whom she had met by chance when she went to buy some medication for her son Steven.

Bruce Goldwyn had two children from a previous marriage. The 10-year age difference did not bother Edith. On the contrary, she felt that he could give her security and the financial basis she needed so much.

Edith and Bruce got married in a small, modest ceremony. Besides her parents, her sister and Steven, there were of course Bruce, his parents and his two children. A couple of dozen friends crowded onto the green lawn after the ceremony and enjoyed the refreshments. The tables were covered with red and white silk fabric - Edith's favorite colors. After the wedding, they went to Los Angeles for their honeymoon and subsequently returned to New York. The idyll continued.

Gradually, almost imperceptibly, Bruce began to come home late in the evenings. Edith's suspicions grew, and she went to the pharmacy one night. At the entrance to the street, she turned off her lights and edged the white Cadillac quietly forward. At that precise moment, she saw Bruce turn off the lights and leave the store. He locked the door quickly and got into a big blue car that was waiting for him at the corner. For a brief moment, when the light in the car went on, Edith saw the profile of a blonde woman - and then the light went out. The car pulled away quickly and Edith returned home. Bruce arrived home three hours later. Edith was sitting and waiting for him on the leather couch in the living room. She was pale, and held a half-empty bottle of whiskey.

When Bruce came in, there was no point even trying to deny anything. He told her everything: He and Ilona Curtis had met in the psychiatrist's waiting room. Bruce had approached Dr. Barton, the well-known hypnotist, of his own volition. He wanted to get rid of tension. Ilona had come to the same place because she wanted to stop smoking. One day, in the waiting room, a conversation developed, following which they met for a cup of coffee.

Their affair ignited like wildfire. It seemed as if they had always known each other. Bruce was the one who first raised the idea of hypnosis, so they each asked Dr. Barton in turn to hypnotize them in an attempt to uncover the secret of their attraction.

A month later, he invited both of them to a joint session and played them a tape that contained things that had been said under the influence of deep hypnosis. They both reported that they had met about three hundred years before. They both spoke words in an ancient Irish dialect and described meeting places they had fixed.

She was a young girl in a small village in Ireland. He was her sweetheart, the fisherman who had gone out to sea one night and not returned. She swore to love him forever, and leaped to her death in the ocean waves from the cliff at the far end of the village.

Ilona and Bruce flew to Ireland for two weeks. The descriptions on the tape matched precisely - down to the last detail. There was no explanation for it. Three months later, they both decided to leave their spouses and to consummate the love that had been snatched away from them the previous time.

Edith sat quietly and listened to Bruce's story. She stayed there for a long time. Until she heard him pack and go out of the front door.

Regarding the belief in reincarnation in Africa, Dr. E. G. Parringer writes:

Reincarnation, to most Africans, is a good thing. It is a return to this sunlit world for a further period of invigorating life. There is little idea of an end to the number of incarnations, or a search for that as desirable. ... On the contrary, it is bad not to be reborn, and childlessness is a great curse because it blocks the channel of rebirth. Hence the great attention devoted to fertility and the continuing popularity of polygamy, for the ancestor is only reincarnated in his own family. ... It is a common practice for the diviner to be called in at the birth of a child to declare which ancestor is reincarnated, and family resemblances are explained as due to use of the same soul-stuff. ...

Various phrases are used to describe reincarnation. One West African people calls it "the shooting forth of a branch," and another "a recurring cycle." In the latter case the same word is used to describe a vine which twines round a post, reappearing continually higher up.

E. G. Parringer, "Varities of Belief in Reincarnation," *The Hibbert Journal*, April 1957

A South American dream

Pnina Cohen first read Erich von Däniken's *Chariots of the Gods* in 1968. The book was new and was creating a sensation. As a 15-year-old girl, Pnina soared on the wings of her imagination and saw herself hiking in Peru, flying over the Plain of Nazca in a helicopter, looking at the gigantic land drawings, and making discoveries that would change the face of the world. Later on came her high-school years, her first love and the army.

Five years later, Pnina reached Peru. She had met her husband, Ricardo, at a military airbase. He was a volunteer soldier and she knew from the beginning that their affair would be serious. Initially, she had misgivings, but after his persistent European-style courtship, she gave in. Love bloomed, and a year later, Ricardo proposed. She accepted. The modest ceremony was held at a synagogue, and within two weeks, they were on their way overseas. After a honeymoon in a fancy hotel, they rented a small apartment not far from where Ricardo's parents lived. They were nice elderly people with whom Pnina could not communicate at all. They did not speak English and she did not know Spanish.

And then Pnina began to wake up at night. She would see visions, just like a movie on television. Every night she saw something else: long skulls with a hole in the left side of the forehead, bizarre drawings on rock walls, temples, and rocky beaches. She began to draw what she had seen and showed her sketches to her husband. From the expression on his face, she realized that he was surprised. They began to travel on weekends. He took her to the temple in Nazca. She easily identified the central square, shaped like seven trapezes, as well as the gigantic drawings of monkeys and rats, the rocky beaches and the flat desert. She felt that she knew each place.

By the time six months had passed, Pnina had learned to speak Spanish. She and Ricardo went to the local Shaman, where, after a special ceremony, he went into a trance and informed her in a confident voice that she had lived there hundreds of years ago. She had been the doctor who had treated patients and had exorcised the evil spirits that possessed them by piercing their skulls on the left side of their foreheads.

Patrick Bowen, who lived in Africa for many years, describes the link between humans and animals in the context of reincarnation:

As a boy, ten or twelve years of age, following my father's wagon through the wild Bushlands of the Northern Transvaal, I gained the friendship of many *Isanusi* (Wise Men) of the Zulus. One of these, Mankanyezi ("the Starry One") said to me, "Within the body is a soul; within the soul is a spark of the *Itongo*, the Universal Spirit. After the death of the body, *Idholozi* (the soul) hovers for a while near the body, and then departs to *Esil-Weni*, the Places of Beasts. This is very different from entering the body of a beast. In *Esilweni*, the soul assumes a shape, part beast and part human. ... After a period, long or short, according to the strength of the animal nature, the soul throws aside its beast-like shape, and moves onward to – a place of rest. There it sleeps, till a time comes when it *dreams* that something to do and learn awaits it on earth; then it awakes, and returns, through the Place of Beasts, to the earth, and is born again as a child. Again and again does the soul travel thus, till at last the man becomes true Man, and his soul, when the body dies, becomes one with the *Itongo*, whence it came."

P. G. Bowen, "The Ancient Wisdom in Africa," *The Theosophist*, August 1927

Going home

Ricki Levin arrived in Johannesburg in 1982, after getting married. Her new husband, Teddy, whose entire family was still in South Africa, insisted that they go work there for two years to save money.

A week before their departure, Ricki managed to fit in a visit to a well-known fortune-teller. "Your home is not here. You will travel far over the sea. You will live among jungles and waterfalls. That is where you belong, you came from there and you will return there..."

Ricki soon forgot the prophecy. She arrived in Johannesburg, and even though her settling-in period took quite a long time, she found herself increasingly in love with the place.

Five years went by. Ricki and Teddy had two sons. The date of their return was postponed over and over again - each time for a different reason. In the meantime, their relationship deteriorated. They were gradually drifting apart, each one occupied with his or her own affairs.

On Saturdays, Ricki began to go sightseeing with her friend Cheryl. On one of those trips, they arrived at a small place on the outskirts of the nearby city: Zulu Village, which featured blacks dressed in traditional costumes, authentic straw huts, stalls laden with souvenirs, and typical African music echoing in the air.

Dozens of camera-toting German and American tourists crowded into the small amphitheater. At three o'clock, after a light meal and several mugs of cold beer, the noise of the drums got louder and suddenly a dance troupe appeared. The performance was stunning: colorful costumes, wild rhythms and songs... At the end of the performance, Ricki and Cheryl went down to the arena and broke into a spontaneous improvised dance. The dancers were amazed, and, in a conversation that developed later on, over a glass of beer, they exchanged information.

One of the dancers, Emily, asked Ricki for her telephone number. They had never seen a white woman dancing like that, and Emily was not ashamed to say so. Ricki, on her side, felt tremendous excitement. She felt the music in her bones and could imitate the characteristic movements of the Zulu dance with impressive accuracy.

On the way home to her big house surrounded by a high white wall in one of the suburbs of Johannesburg, Ricki was very quiet. That night, she had trouble falling asleep. That's it, I've come home, she felt deep inside herself. She had never experienced such a fierce feeling of belonging.

She stayed at home for two weeks. At the end of the third week, she could no longer restrain herself, and she went back to the place, alone, where she knew the troupe was performing. The members of the troupe received her with applause, and she danced with them again. Once more, she felt a feeling of sublime happiness and satisfaction, as if her life had been fulfilled in those moments. From that weekend on, for six months, she became the troupe's attraction. A white woman, dressed in traditional Zulu costume, dancing with the blacks and singing their songs. She felt that she belonged to the group of dancers, and got to know them personally - the name and life history of each one.

When her friend Emily suggested that she join her for a week to visit her family, it was impossible for Ricki to refuse. They traveled all night in a small van. In the morning, Ricki awoke to a bright day on the banks of a large lake surrounded by dense jungle. The little curly-haired children, the black men and women, all looked curiously at the white woman who was so thin. They tugged at her long blonde hair, until she finally plaited it into two braids. Again, Ricki felt the same powerful feeling of déjà vu. Although she was so different from them, she belonged here... she had grown up here...

In the evening, around the campfire, in the middle of the village, she met the Sangoma, the witch doctor of the village. Her friend from the troupe translated his words: "You were born here and lived here in a previous incarnation. Now you have come home; we have been waiting for you..."

A week went by, and when they returned to the big city, they decided to rent an apartment together. Ricki went home to pack her bags. Her husband did not have much to say. The children stayed with him, and she went to live in a two-room apartment in the center of Johannesburg. Once a month, Ricki went to the village, and it was there that she remembered the prophecy of the fortune-teller: "Your home is not here... You will live among jungles and waterfalls..."

The protagonist of Christopher Marlowe's *Doctor Faustus* laments the fact that he will never be reincarnated as an animal, according to the Pythagorean belief:

Ah, Pythagoras' metempsychosis! were that true,
   This soul should fly from me and I be changed
   Into some brutish beast! all beasts are happy,
   For when they die,
   Their souls are soon dissolved in elements;
   But mine must live, still to be plagued in hell.

Christopher Marlowe, *Doctor Faustus*

A trip to America

The Afutas had planned their trip to America for ten years. They were both Israelis, and they had never left the country, although they were both 30.

They had met during their military service at a base in the south of the country. Love bloomed in the desert.

In August 1966, when Avi Afuta was about to be discharged from the Israel Defense Forces, he proposed to Ofira on a moonlit night. She accepted happily. The parents on both sides pooled their resources and bought the young couple a small two-room apartment in a quiet street in Bat Yam as a wedding present. In a daring move, Avi Afuta borrowed 400 liras from his parents and bought a simple knitting machine. He worked day and night, went from store to store in the city, and sold his merchandise. Within six months, Avi had already moved to a larger place in the Tel Aviv industrial area. He set up two knitting machines in a corner of the large warehouse and began to work energetically. His wife Ofira came to help him. As time passed, the business grew and their bank account swelled. They even managed to save a handsome sum of several thousand dollars.

Ten years went by. Lior and Hagit, the twins who had been born two years after their marriage, were already eight years old. Avi and Ofira Afuta decided to make their lifetime dream come true: they left their children with Grandma Hannah and took off for New York on a rainy winter's day.

After a long and exhausting flight, the plane landed in New York, in the middle of a snowstorm. The representatives of the organized tour bundled the group of cold and tired Israelis into a bus, which drove them to a rustic motel about 15 minutes' drive from the airport.

The plan was to spend the night there and to go on to the Holiday Inn the next morning. After checking in, Ofira and Avi were allocated a small, old room on the second floor. The room was furnished simply with heavy wooden furniture: a bed, two chests of drawers, and a closet with three doors. The middle door featured a large mirror.

They left their suitcases open, grabbed the bare minimum for the brief overnight stay, showered, and quickly got into bed.

The snowstorm continued the whole of the next day and even increased in intensity. The group members found themselves stuck in the little hotel. Between meals, most of them were happy to catch up on sleep.

Avi and Ofira woke up late. They went down to the restaurant, ate, and returned to their room immediately afterwards. They fell fast asleep immediately. At a certain point, Avi woke up, drenched in sweat. The room was in semi-darkness and he did not know what the time was. All he knew was that he had had the strangest dream. He saw himself wearing a strange military uniform and a large hat. A large gun hung on his belt. He saw himself standing in front of a mirror and saying: "Look for the treasure behind you! There's a lot of money there!" Avi woke up in a fright. He got up and went to the bathroom, washed his face and shaved. While he was looking at the reflection of his face in the mirror, he wiped off the rest of the shaving foam and suddenly understood.

With a pounding heart, he ran to the suitcase and took a pen-knife out of a small plastic travel-bag. He hurried to the closet in the other room. The four small screws squeaked under the pressure of his nimble hand. He quickly removed the mirror and placed it carefully on the wooden floor.

Behind a thin layer of yellowing newspapers in the hollow inside the thick door, he saw shining gold bars arranged in rows.

Ofira woke up and looked at her husband in amazement as he removed 30 gold bars from the closet door. Avi had just replaced the large mirror when there was a knock at the door. The tour guide had come to call them to go out. Avi and Ofira did not go anywhere that day. They called a cab and went to deposit the gold in a nearby bank.

Every year for the next ten years, the couple arrived in New York. They bought an apartment on Fifth Avenue, and stayed there during their visits. They expanded the business in Tel Aviv until it became the leader in the industry.

Success smiled on them. No one understood how they had made money and become one of the richest couples in the country.

The only souvenir they kept of that fateful trip to the United States was a page or two of yellowing newsprint...

In the dialogue, *Meno*, Plato quotes Socrates on the immortality of the soul:

Socrates: I have heard from certain wise men and women who spoke ... of a glorious truth, as I conceive.

Meno: What was it? and who were they?

Socrates: Some of them were priests and priest-esses, who had studied how they might be able to give a reason [for] their profession: there have been poets also, who spoke of these things by inspiration, like Pindar, and many others who were inspired. And they say – mark, now, and see whether their words are true – they say that the soul of man is immortal, and at one time has an end, which is termed dying, and at another time is born again, but is never destroyed. And the moral is, that a man ought to live always in perfect holiness. ...

The soul, then, as being immortal, and having been born again many times, and having seen all things that exist, whether in this world or in the world below, has knowledge of them all; and it is no wonder that she should be able to call to remembrance all that she ever knew about virtue, and about everything; for as all nature is akin, and the soul has learned all things, there is no difficulty in her eliciting or as men say learning, out of a single recollection all the rest, if a man is strenuous and does not faint; for all enquiry and all learning is but recollection.

Dialogues of Plato, translated by Jowett (1937)

A white death

Francine McNey was widowed at age 50. Her late husband, Jerry, who had been a wealthy businessman, left her a great deal of money. She knew that she would never have to worry about supporting herself, even if their son Jeff didn't help her. Jeff had left the house at age 20 as part of his adolescent revolt. He had gone to Los Angeles and become rich there. Once a year he would come and visit in a fancy flashy car, each time with another bimbo hanging on his arm. He was always angry and in a foul mood. After trying to placate him for years, his parents had given up. They decided to spend their lives enjoying themselves.

Jerry and Francine traveled all over the world. Every two or three months, Jerry would leave his offices in the hands of his skilled staff and get on a plane with his lovely wife to another destination. They visited the Far East, the Caribbean Islands, New Zealand and Australia. In the last two years, they returned to Switzerland. They had been there for the first time three years before and had fallen in love with the tranquil atmosphere of the snowy Alps. The perfect place, in their opinion, was Davos. It was an enchanted place that attracted intrepid skiers from all over the world. In a short time, Francine and Jerry became accomplished skiers. They bought the most advanced equipment and the best and most attractive clothes.

While the two of them were skiing down the snowy slopes of the resort, it was impossible not to admire their impressive performance. They were not particularly young - they were both approaching 50 - but there was no doubt that they knew how to enjoy life to the full.

The third time they returned to Switzerland for a white vacation, as Jerry called it, Francine had a bad feeling. Her initial enthusiasm waned when two days before the trip, Jerry's mother, Kate, appeared in a dream. She was trying to push her son to one side and save him, but to no avail. In seconds, they were both buried under a large avalanche...

Francine woke up screaming in terror. Jerry got up and went to the kitchen to get her a glass of warm milk. He calmed her down, and after he had heard the story, burst out laughing. He reminded her that he had lived in an orphanage until age ten and did not know his biological mother at all. His adoptive parents lived in good health and comfort in a fancy senior citizens' home in Pennsylvania, not far from where Francine and Jerry lived. So there was no need to worry...

In retrospect, Francine was sorry that she had not taken her intuition more seriously. The third trip to Davos in Switzerland became their last trip together. During their last week there, Jerry went skiing in the early afternoon. It was a lovely, bright, sunny day. Francine preferred to stay in the heated room, read a book and rest. When Jerry still hadn't returned at five o'clock, Francine began to worry. She went down to the hotel reception and then she saw the worried faces of the clerks. An avalanche - that was all she heard. When she told them in a trembling voice that her husband was somewhere on the slope, she knew that the very worst had happened. Nothing and nobody could escape a huge avalanche, which buries everything in its path under dozens of meters of compressed snow.

Things were organized rapidly. Guides and rescue workers went out on a search that continued far into the night, but it was futile. After a crazy sleepless night, Francine joined the search party in the morning. After about three more hours of searching with the help of specially trained dogs, Jerry's frozen body was found. After she had recovered from the initial shock, Francine requested that Jerry be buried in the local cemetery. She thought that he would have liked the idea of his grave being situated at the top of a snowy hill in the pastoral silence of the Alps.

What she didn't expect to find in the cemetery in Davos, Switzerland, was an old grave with the faded inscription:

Here lies Kate McNey

who perished in 1939

in an avalanche

The German poet, J. W. von Goethe (1749-1832), was deeply interested in reincarnation:

I am certain that I have been here as I am now a thousand times before, and I hope to return a thousand times. ... Respecting ourselves, however, it almost seems that our previous sojourns were too commonplace to deserve a second thought in the eyes of nature. ... I cannot deny that there may be higher natures than our own among the Monads [Souls]. A World-Monad may produce out of the womb of its memories that which will prove prophetic but is actually a dim remembrance of something long expired. Similarly, human genius in a lightning flash of recollection can discover the laws involved in producing the universe, because it was present when those laws were established.

As quoted in *Memoirs of Johannes Falk* (1832)

A hot death

Penelope Ligasay arrived in Pompeii for the first time in 1960 when she was 19. It was her only visit to the city where thousands of people had died in a volcanic eruption. She visited Pompeii briefly with the person who would become her husband - Antonio Dabos, a young architect from Naples. The moment they arrived in Pompeii, Penelope felt bad. She smelled an odor of sulfur, even though no one else on the tour bus knew what she was talking about. Antonio tried to be as considerate and delicate as he could, but she did not make it easy for him. She was plagued by restlessness and insisted that the two of them go on the tour alone, without the rest of the group.

When the others had moved away, Penelope took Antonio's hand in hers and told him in a trembling voice: "Follow me." She led him to one of the alleys in which there were figures frozen in lava. When they reached the remains of a particular building, she said: "I lived here; those are my parents and that's me." She pointed at three fossilized corpses - two adults and a baby.

Penelope burst into tears and Antonio hugged her and held her tightly against his chest. What else could he do? He suggested that they leave the place, and that's what they did. Penelope remained silent the whole way back. The visit to Pompeii had been traumatic for her. Never, she thought, would she go back to that place where fate had struck her and her family down.

Penelope forgot about Pompeii and the distant past. She continued her studies, married Antonio and had three children.

At age 40, when the children had grown up, she went to Colombia on a diplomatic mission with her husband. The duration of their planned sojourn there was three years, with frequent visits to Italy. Their stay in the Armaro region of Colombia was more successful than Penelope could ever have imagined. The people, the scenery and the work - she loved everything. She requested an extension. The Italian Foreign Office granted her request. She succeeded in developing extensive and profitable commercial ties for both countries. Everyone was happy. The mission was extended for another three years.

In 1985, the Armaro volcano in Colombia erupted. The streams of molten lava killed 23,000 people. Among the dead were Penelope, a representative of the Italian Foreign Office, and her husband, Antonio, the well-known architect.

The Swiss physician and alchemist, Paracelsus (1493-1541), expresses his views as follows:

Some children are born from heaven, and others are born from hell, because each human being has his inherent tendencies, and these tendencies belong to his spirit, and indicate the state in which he existed before he was born. Witches and sorcerers are not made at once; they are born with powers for evil. The body is only an instrument; if you seek for man in his dead body, you are seeking for him in vain. ... The form may be destroyed; but the spirit remains and is living, for it is the subjective life. ...

The body which we receive from our parents ... has no spiritual powers, for wisdom and virtue, faith, hope and charity, do not grow from the earth. These powers are not the products of man's physical organization, but the attributes of another invisible and glorified body, whose germs are laid within man. The physical body changes and dies, the glorified body is eternal. This eternal man is the real man, and is not generated by his earthly parents. He does not draw nutriment from the earth, but from the eternal invisible source from which he originated. ... The temporal body is the house of the eternal, and we should therefore take care of it, because he who destroys the temporal body destroys the house of the eternal, and although the eternal man is invisible, he exists nevertheless, and will become visible in time.

As quoted in Franz Hartmann, *The Life of Philippus Theophrastus Bombast of Hohenheim* (1959)

500 meters beneath
the surface of the earth

Kevin McKay simply knew that he had lived in Mexico in the past. It was as clear as the nose on his face. He just didn't know when and where.

In 1987, the Lachugia cave was opened for the first time, somewhere in the dark depths under the mountains of Mexico: 150 kilometers of underground tunnels, a temperature of 20 degrees Celsius, and high humidity in the sulfur-saturated compressed air. Despite the difficult conditions, the first explorers excitedly reported gigantic stalactites like chandeliers, and deep crevices, more serrated and impressive than any others they had ever seen.

Kevin McKay read the article in the scientific journal he received as a lecturer in archeology at the University of Florida. The very next day he requested an appointment with the dean, and at the end of the semester, took a direct flight to Mexico.

He took a cab from the airport to the home of his old friend, Dale Asivado. The two had first met at an archeological conference in 1985. Since then, they had kept in touch by letter and annual meetings. Dale was slightly surprised to receive an excited telephone call from his friend Kevin, but unhesitatingly agreed to host him in his home.

That same evening, after they had eaten dinner in a fancy restaurant in the city, Dale understood the reason for the unexpected visit. Two weeks before reading the article about the Lachugia cave, Kevin had begun to have weird dreams. He dreamed about his father and mother, who had been dead for a long time. Go home, they said, Go to Lachugia. Kevin was surprised. He had never heard of this place, and his parents had lived their entire lives in Canada. He himself had only left Canada at age 25, when he completed his studies at the University of Toronto. The barren, mountainous desert was not the home he knew. Two weeks after the dreams had begun, he saw the article about the discovery of the cave. Kevin understood the connection immediately. He told his friend Dale about his feeling that he had lived in Mexico some time in the past. Now the pieces of the puzzle were beginning to come together.

Within three months, Kevin and Dale had obtained a substantial budget that would allow them to organize a well-equipped team. It took three more months to find the right people.

At the beginning of 1988, the five members of the group stood at the opening of the cave in southern Mexico: Kevin, Dale, Penelope, Chris and Jack. Hard hats with attached flashlights and rucksacks with food and first-aid supplies were the only things they could take with them.

Kevin went in first. He simply felt that he knew the cave from the inside. Since was the head of the team, none of the members but Dale suspected that he had any other motives besides pure archeological interest.

For the first time in his life, Kevin knew the truth. Already on the first night, he had a dream in which he saw a small tribe of cave residents. Wild animals, figures of wolves, had made him and his father flee to the mouth of the Luchagia cave. The women and the men who were wrapped in furs left the cave at the beginning of the difficult summer. They went off to another place in a desperate attempt to find food, and they never returned to the cave...

Kevin awoke from the dream sweating from excitement. He was excited when he understood that he had finally returned to the cave in which he had lived in that distant era. After five days in the depths of the earth, additional paths were marked in the limestone earth, taking great care not to damage the stunning underground scenery.

Kevin McKay is still wandering around the silent paths among the mountains of Mexico. He stayed in the place where he feels he belongs.

Ralph Waldo Emerson (1803-1882) was an American philosopher and essayist who subscribed to the notion of reincarnation:

It is the secret of the world that all things subsist and do not die, but only retire a little from sight and afterwards return again. ... Nothing is dead; men feign themselves dead, and endure mock funerals and mournful obituaries, and there they stand looking out of the window, sound and well, in some new strange disguise. Jesus is not dead; he is very well alive; nor John, nor Paul, nor Mahomet, nor Aristotle; at times we believe we have seen them all, and could easily tell the names under which they go.

R. W. Emerson, *"Nominalist and Realist"*

The resurrection of the king-god

The Hindu religion is ruled by Shiva, the god who destroys and resurrects, and the resurrection of the king-god, which plays a central role in every topic regarding rebirth. Hindu mythology includes cosmic processes, among them the death and rebirth of races and cultures: the world was created holy and perfect. During the first period, which was called the Golden Age, everything went smoothly. Gradually things began to deteriorate, until, four long periods later, the world was ready for destruction by means of the dancing feet of the god Shiva. This is not the end of the world; it is created anew with the smile of the old Shiva.

Support for the opinion that the universe has been destroyed and recreated an infinite number of times has been found among scientists and astronomers in recent years. There is a claim that the cosmos is shrinking and expanding in a kind of symbolic "heartbeat", exploding once every 82 billion years, destroying and giving life to countless new stars.

The sun, which disappears and appears every day in accordance with the seasons, represents the fixed cyclical character of nature. Jung related to the subject in his book, *Man and His Symbols*. At age 83, Jung conceived this book and spent the last months of his life writing it.

In his book, *Ancient Mythologies and Modern Man*, Joseph Anderson wrote: "We read the mythology of ancient Greece, or the folk legends of the Indians in America, but we do not succeed in linking them with the approach of modern man to the 'heroes' or dramatic events of today."

Even though the link may sometimes be hidden, it does exist. The symbols are important and significant to humanity. Anyone who has received a Christian education is certainly familiar with several important examples. At Christmas, the birth of the holy child is celebrated, even if we do not believe in the virgin who gave birth to a son, or if we are not especially religious. Without being aware of it, we have accepted the influence of a sign of rebirth. This is an old cycle of festivities that inspire hope, for after the cold winter that afflicts the northern hemisphere comes the spring, bearing renewal on its wings. With all the modernization and sophistication, we all love the symbols that exist in the festivals throughout the year and in all cultures.

Do we understand what we are doing, or do we see the link between the birth of Jesus, death and Easter? In general, we do not think in that manner, or we analyze our actions from a philosophical point of view. The crucifixion of Jesus is parallel to the stories described in mythology with regard to other gods: Osiris, Tammuz, Orpheus, or the biblical story of Joseph in Egypt. They were also considered saints when they were born, since their births occurred in incredible circumstances. They flourished, became leaders, were executed, and were subsequently resurrected. They belong to religions in which the death and resurrection of the king-god constitute an inseparable part.

The German philosopher and mathematician, Leibniz (1646-1716), expounded his views on reincarnation in the following passage:

As animals are usually not born completely in conception or generation, so neither do they perish completely in what we call death; for it is reasonable that what does not begin naturally should not come to an end in the order of nature either. Thus, casting off their masks or their rags, they merely return to a more subtle scene, on which, however, they can be as sensible and as well ordered as on the greater one. ... Thus not only souls but animals also are ingenerable and imperishable; they are only developed, enveloped, reclad, stripped, transformed; souls never leave the whole of their body, and do not pass from one body to another which is entirely new to them. Thus there is no metempsychosis, but there is metamorphosis.

Leibniz, *Principles of Nature*

Psycho and the butterfly

The goddess Psycho, to whom we owe the root of the word *psychology*, was one of the names given by the Greeks to the soul in ancient times. The symbol of the goddess Psycho, like that the soul, was a butterfly. The symbolism that exists here is clear and well known.

Everyone is familiar with the wonderful metamorphosis of a larva into a butterfly, but only a few people are aware of the fact that the larva goes through three to four stages, during the course of which it sheds its skin several times, and changes beyond recognition. Only a professional biologist can identify the creature that changes its appearance completely. After the "death sleep", a beautiful butterfly emerges, and without the proof of having witnessed it directly, it would be impossible to believe or even conceive of the fact that it developed from the pupa.

Undoubtedly, metamorphosis and reincarnation are two completely different processes. The first consists of a gradual but significant change in a particular form, while the second involves an absolutely new development. Despite the difference between them, these two ideas have always been intermeshed. In the opinion of many people, the stories of Greek and Roman mythology also represent these ideas.

In modern psychology, the inner eternal nature of human beings was ignored for years. The psycho was considered to be the "mind" and mental processes with no relation to the soul.

In Erich Fromm's opinion, the fact that the soul was forgotten somewhere in the process of the development of this science meant that there was something missing in it. In time, there were people in this profession who broadened their horizons and introduced elements from the East into Western psychology, thus reinforcing the belief in reincarnation.

The views of the famous American statesman, scientist and philosopher, Benjamin Franklin, on reincarnation are evident in the following passages, the first of which is an epitaph he composed for himself at age 22:

The Body of B. Franklin,
Printer,
Like the Cover of an Old Book,
Its Contents Torn Out
And
Stripped of its Lettering and Gilding,
Lies Here
Food for Worms,
But the Work shall not be Lost,
For it Will as He Believed
Appear Once More
In a New and more Elegant Edition
Revised and Corrected
By the Author.

His later views were apparently unchanged:
When I see nothing annihilated and not a drop of water wasted, I cannot suspect the annihilation of souls, or believe that [God] will suffer the daily waste of millions of minds ready made that now exist, and put Himself to the continual trouble of making new ones. Thus, finding myself to exist in the world, I believe I shall, in some shape or other, always exist; and, with all the inconveniences human life is liable to, I shall not object to a new edition of mine, hoping, however, that the *errata* of the last may be corrected.

Benjamin Franklin, Letter to George Whatley, May 23, 1785

Shopping in the market

At age 18, Lily Ravid married Yigael. He took her to his parents' home in Jaffa (Israel), where they lived until the birth of their two children. During that time, Yigael's father became ill. The little house was filled with medical equipment and the odor of medications. For the first time in her life, Lily decided to put her foot down. After dinner, she washed the dishes, walked into the living-room, stood in front of the TV set, and announced: "We're moving." Her husband and his parents were stunned.

Lily herself did not know where the strength to dig in her heels had come from. From the first day she had known Yigael, she had felt a compulsive need to give in to him on every single thing. The situation only became worse after their wedding. She became the cook, the cleaner and later the caregiver. Deep inside her, her feeling of bitterness increased, but she never dared to raise her voice or oppose Yigael or his parents - not, that is, until that evening, in front of the TV, when for the first time she dared to hold her head up high and express her own wishes.

The cause of the change that had taken place in her had begun several months previously. One Thursday, when Lily was on her way home from the market, a small black car stopped near her. The driver, a religious man with a black beard, offered her a ride. Lily, feeling the weight of the packages she was carrying, succumbed to the temptation. She got into the car and got out at the corner of the street where she lived. In the weeks that followed, Lily and Itzik, the driver, met twice more. On their third meeting, the conversation took a more personal turn.

Itzik, who turned out to be a newly religious psychologist, suggested that Lily undergo a few sessions of treatment. After a few sessions, when she lay back in the big soft chair that was meant for his clients, Itzik taught her how to relax. She closed her eyes and imagined herself walking along a mountain path, free of all the tension she suffered from on a daily basis. Itzik's voice continued to accompany her in the first part of the relaxation process and afterwards fell silent. Lily saw herself clearly in an old-fashioned wooden cabin built. "Gilda! Gilda!" She heard a man's voice calling, and when she turned around, she saw a tall, fair man glaring at her angrily. At that moment, she heard an infant crying loudly. Gilda ran and held the infant in her arms until it had calmed down. The man spat out a few rapid sentences, lifted up a large heavy bag, and left the house. Gilda knew that he was going to look for food. She also knew that she would be left alone for a long time with a small hungry baby and no food. She got dressed, dressed her baby son, and walked along a forest path for three hours until she reached the big market. She sold the big warm scarf she loved so much and bought a little food. That night, she went to sleep early. The walk home was very long and she was tired. At some point before dawn, Gilda woke up with a feeling of acute anxiety. She heard inexplicable noises. From beneath the straw mattress, she pulled out a long knife that she had hidden there long ago for this precise purpose.

The moment the door opened, Gilda plunged the knife into the invader's body. A scream rang out and then the moaning figure sank to the floor. Gilda quickly lit the oil lamp. On the floor, lying in his own blood, was her husband. He managed to give her an inquiring look and then closed his eyes forever.

Lily opened her eyes. It took her a few moments to digest what had been revealed to her while she had been in another dimension. She trembled and began to cry. She also suddenly understood the mass of guilt feelings, her endless and compulsive need to give in, and her constant need to please her husband; but she also understood that now she had finished paying her debts to the man who was her husband then, and now...

Jean Paul Richter (1763-1825), the famous German novelist who exerted a great influence on the writers of his time, as well as on the composer Robert Schumann, wrote about reincarnation:

The least valid objection to the theory of soul-circulation is that we forget these journeyings. Even during this life and without experiencing a "change of clothes," multifarious conditions vanish from our memories. How then should we expect to remember the different bodies and the still more varied conditions experienced in previous lives? Why not allow a way of thinking to enjoy full light that a Plato, a Pythagoras, and whole nations and eras have not disdained? ... Let the soul return as often as it wishes. Certainly the earth is rich enough to bestow ever new gifts, new centuries, new countries, new minds, new discoveries and hopes.

J. P. Richter, *Selina*

The double murder

Twenty-eight-year-old Dr. Oland Hensen had lived in Denmark all his life. That evening, in 1959, he arrived home earlier than expected. When he went into the bedroom, he saw his wife Johanna naked in bed with a dark-skinned stranger. He didn't have time to think. He pulled out the Beretta he always wore in his belt and fired... The bed was covered with blood, and the bodies of the man and the woman lay lifeless on the once-white sheets. The affair remained headline news for a few weeks. The Danish police searched for Dr. Hensen for months, but he was very far away from there. That same bitter night, he had grabbed a few personal belongings and gotten onto the first plane out of Denmark.

The gigantic Boeing landed in Rio de Janeiro, Brazil. Hensen disappeared into the crowd, which had been celebrating the carnival for a week. Juanita Cabalo was only 19 when she met Dr. Hensen that fateful week. She took him home and gave him food and shelter, and then all the love in the world. Two months later, they held a wedding reception at the home of Juanita's parents, to the sounds of Brazilian music.

A year later, their daughter was born. They called her Jonina at Juanita's request. As the child grew up, she resembled Johanna more and more closely. Hensen did not understand how this was possible.

Twenty years passed. In addition to Jonina, the couple had

three more children - who resembled their mother, Juanita. There were many guests at Jonina's twentieth birthday party, as well as music, dancing and food. Everyone agreed that it was a great party. Late that night, when everything was over, Oland Hensen went into his study. He sat there quietly and listened to classical music, as was his habit. This was what he always did when he was upset and irritated. Jonina was a woman now. More than ever she looked and behaved like Johanna. She had the same blue eyes, wavy blond hair and charming movement of her head when she laughed. On the night of her birthday, he remembered the full intensity of the pain and madness he had felt that fateful night when he killed Johanna and her lover.

Numerous questions rose up in his mind, questions he had never thought about before: Who was the dark-skinned man he had found in bed with his wife that day? Was it a one-off affair or were they having a long-standing relationship? The act of betrayal was unforgivable, from his point of view, but did it have to end in death?

Oland Hensen shook off these thoughts when he heard a soft knock at the door. It was Jonina. They had never gotten along, so he was surprised when she came to his study. "I wanted to thank you for the party," she said, smiling. Oland Hensen was surprised. He hugged her and suggested that they have a cup of tea together. When Hensen went to the kitchen, Jonina quickly pulled a small box out of the pocket of her silk robe. She took out a single cyanide pill and quickly dissolved it in her father's tea...

A month after the funeral, Jonina returned to Denmark.

The German philosopher, Friedrich von Schlegel (1772-1829), studied oriental languages and wrote philosophical works that dealt with reincarnation:

Philosophy has primarily to refute two basic errors: firstly, that the human soul can dissolve into nothingness, and secondly, that man, without any effort of his own, is already fully endowed with immortality. ... Man as he is now is entirely too imperfect, too material, to claim that higher kind of immortality. He will have to enter into other earthly, yet far more refined and transfigured forms and developments before he can directly partake of the eternal glory of the divine world of light. ...

The idea of metempsychosis, embraced by mysticism, is remarkable in itself for its antiquity. ... It does not permit the soul to pass to full freedom before it has incarnated in many bodies. Here we view metempsychosis in its most general meaning as continuance of spirit, alternately using organic forms, and not in the sense of ... an aggravating punishment ever accelerating.

F. von Schlegel, *Cologne Lectures (1804-1806)*

The return of the gods,
or who contributed what to reincarnation

For years, archeologists have been occupied with attempts to solve the great mysteries of the ancient world. How were the pyramids built? Who gave the ancients their great knowledge in the fields of medicine and astronomy? There are many questions, but the answers are still shrouded in uncertainty.

Mythology tells of gods that intervened in human life during what is called "the Golden Age". During this period, people learned everything the gods taught them in the realms of art and science, and then the gods left, promising to return when necessary. During this period, the whole of humanity lived in harmony. They spoke the same language and shared the same belief and the same universal truth. When the gods left, things gradually began to deteriorate.

Scientists tend to scoff at mythological stories like this. However, today, more than ever, there are scientists who suggest that the most feasible explanation lies in the existence of intelligent and developed beings that live in the universe and once took an active part in the development of life on earth.

The approach that supports reincarnation perceives in these creatures or beings a phenomenon of evolutionary development through many incarnations of life and worlds. A few decades ago, it was Erich von

Däniken who popularized the theory that gods from outer space had come down or returned to earth as astronauts in spaceships. In the myths, Hiawatha promised his people that he would return, as did Wiracoca in the Inca culture, Kuatez in the Aztec culture, and King Arthur in England.

In the Far East, the avatar theory is studied. This is the belief in the incarnation of God or lofty beings who are beyond rebirth. Krishna, Buddha, Lao-Tse and other saints who reached the highest and final level are examples of such beings. The Hindus are waiting for Kalki-Otar, the Buddhists are waiting for Buddha, the Zoroastrians are waiting for Susiosh, the Muslims are waiting for Imam, the Jews are waiting for the Messiah (some surmise that he was the first man, and afterwards David), and the Christians are waiting for the second coming of Jesus.

Many people think that when the great "order", according to which things run, goes wrong, the gods will come and establish a new order. Many think that our ailing world, which is torn apart by wars, social problems, famine and illness, as well as by other problems, is in need of the return of the gods as soon as possible. As Krishna says, "I come down to the creatures when I see decay, deterioration, injustice… and thus I incarnate from generation to generation… to look after the just… to destroy the evil, and to uphold the righteous…"

A similar notion can be found in the New Testament, where Jesus talks about his second coming: "The time will come when nations will fight each other. There will be drought and famine and earthquakes in many places. That is how the new generation will begin – the new time." He is not talking about the end of the world, as many people think.

The idea of "the return of the gods" also appears in modern theosophy, and is linked to what is called "the lords of wisdom", who choose to come back to earth after their death in order to help the human race develop to the extent that its karma will permit. The accepted version is that the gods never really left. They are in our world, and continue to work with humanity.

In his book, *The Ocean of Theosophy*, William Q. Dedadge described humanity as being accompanied by friends – older brothers – that help it develop. They safeguard the knowledge that has accumulated throughout the years and wait for a suitable opportunity to contribute to the development of knowledge on earth as well as in other places in the universe.

"The older brothers" are souls that have perfected themselves during the periods of evolution. In certain periods, they lived among simple people in places that permitted them to live there. If they had revealed themselves in all their greatness, they would immediately have become objects of worship like gods. In certain cases, some of them did indeed reveal themselves as teachers, guides or philosophers, while others remained anonymous.

There are ancient stories about these people. Such stories existed in the king's court in ancient Egypt; they are mentioned in the story of Apollonius. Abraham and Moses, members of the Jewish religion, also belong to that group. Other heroes of this kind are, of course, Buddha, Confucius and Jesus.

In the Sanskrit language, there is a word that relates to these figures: matma. Translated freely, mat means greatness and atma means soul. The greatness of these people is rooted in the "size" of their soul. The notion of matma is liable to appear contrived in the view of many people, but it is reinforced if reincarnation is indeed recognized as one of the laws of nature.

During the course of one period of life, the aspiration to perfection is practically an impossible mission. The experience accumulated during entire periods of life can turn each person into "God". It is said about Buddha: "This is the blooming of the human tree, which blossoms after many years, and when this happens, the world is filled with the fragrance of wisdom."

According to the Hindu religion, human life is a long journey that continues not only from cradle to grave, but extends over millions of years. The spiritual being continues to exist during the time when nations rise and fall, and the environment changes. Existence begins from a shining spot that detaches itself from the central fire and gains momentum and experience in the course of different lives. The person fulfills different functions: once he is a king, once he is a slave. He goes up and down the rungs of the ladder, each time changing his identity and his image.

As stated previously, the notion of rebirth is widespread in the East. The philosophers and the teachers of religion have never felt the need to prove this approach, since it has always been an inseparable part of the local culture. What interests the people of the East is the search for the way to liberate oneself from the inevitable suffering that the process of rebirth entails, and that ultimately leads to spiritual enlightenment, freedom and – finally – nirvana.

The West has had difficulty accepting this approach. The original texts of the Hindu and Buddhist religions stressed the need to separate between what the great scholars in the East taught and the later development of achieving nirvana as the supreme objective of man's aspirations. A certain contradiction exists between the philosophy of reincarnation and living in that wonderful place – nirvana – man's final, ultimate objective in his many incarnations on earth.

In the infinite universe, there must be infinite possibilities for growth and wisdom, self-realization and the expansion of awareness, as well as the development of the qualities of compassion and the ability to sacrifice. To this end, man has to exist as a person.

The Vedas are the most ancient writings ever unearthed in India. All the traditions agree that these writings stem from the region around Manasrobra Lake in Tibet. These writings are extremely ancient, dating back further than the cultures of Egypt, Israel, Greece, Rome, Inca and Maya, and they attest to an extremely developed culture. It is very important to study the nature of reincarnation as it appears in this source.

The philosopher and scholar Radahkrishnan, who was once the president of India, wrote that the notion of reincarnation appears in even earlier writings: "The soul's journey out of the body is found in other forms of existence. The soul returns to the human body according to the principles of karma."

David Lloyd George (1863-1945), who served as the prime minister of Britain from 1916 to 1922, described his sentiments about reincarnation as follows:

When I was a boy, the thought of Heaven used to frighten me more than the thought of Hell. I pictured Heaven as a place where there would be perpetual Sundays with perpetual services, from which there would be no escape, as the Almighty, assisted by cohorts of angels, would always be on the look-out for those who did not attend. It was a horrible nightmare.

The conventional Heaven with its angels perpetually singing, etc., nearly drove me mad in my youth and made me an atheist for ten years. My opinion is that we shall be reincarnated ... and that hereafter we shall suffer or benefit in accordance with that we have done in this world. For example, the employer who sweats his workpeople will be condemned to be sweated himself.

As quoted in *Lord Riddell's Intimate Diary of the Peace Conference and After* (1933)

A nun in the basement

Malcolm Price and his wife Marian were in their early twenties when they arrived in the Scilly Isles, opposite the southern coast of England. The two youngsters had met and fallen in love in London. After a modest wedding, they decided to move to a rural area, and they chose the Scilly Isles. They purchased a large plot of land at a low price and built their house on the hill near the bank of a river, on the ruins of an ancient building.

They lived happily for seven years. They had five children. They grew vegetables and raised domestic animals. Hens and cows provided fresh eggs and milk every day. Then, one day, without any warning, the nightmare began. That day, all the members of the family had gone off to their rooms earlier than usual, and when they were all sound asleep, Malcolm and Marian were woken at midnight by the sound of weeping. They checked the children's rooms over and over again, but the children were all sleeping peacefully.

When the phenomenon recurred, the couple turned to the local priest, Joseph Stuart. He suggested that they check the church register. After they had gone down to the basement and taken the old books out, the following facts came to light: In 1800, a young nun by the name of Virginia Hest lived in the local convent. She became involved in a forbidden love affair with one of the villagers - Lawrence Campbell. The man lived in the house that stood in exactly the same place as Malcolm and Marian Price's house now stood.

Lawrence and Virginia fell in love. She decided to leave the convent for him, but then discovered that she was pregnant. Lawrence's conservative parents did not agree to welcome her into their family. One winter night, she stood for hours knocking on the gates of her lover's big estate. He was locked in his room and could not help her. His heartless parents ignored her.

Snow began to fall - soft, lovely flakes that piled up into a white carpet and covered the whole village. In the morning, she was found lying next to the gate, frozen to death. Her body was buried in a field next to the convent.

The broken-hearted Lawrence left his home with no intention of ever returning... He returned many years later, however, after his parents had died. Five years later, he died of a serious illness and was buried in the family burial plot.

Malcolm and Marian returned home stunned. Now they understood what the weeping meant. On the advice of the priest, they went to the field next to the convent where, behind a thorny green hedge, they found the graveyard. Virginia Hest's name was engraved on one of the old tombstones.

A week later, a small truck drove up to the graveyard, carrying several people dressed in black. Using special equipment, they exhumed Virginia's bones and reburied them next to her beloved Lawrence - in the family burial plot.

The sound of weeping that was heard at night in Malcolm and Marian's house ceased.

At a certain point, Leo Tolstoy (1828-1910), the Russian novelist and social and religious philosopher, grappled with what he perceived as the futility of life and the problem of committing suicide. He discussed the latter in the following passage:

How interesting it would be to write the story of the experiences in this life of a man who killed himself in his previous life; how he now stumbles against the very demands which had offered themselves before, until he arrives at the realization that he must fulfil those demands. Remembering the lesson, this man will be wiser than others.

L. Tolstoy, *My Confession*

The forest-keeper

The winter of 1795 in Tampere, Finland, was one of the harshest the region had ever experienced - at least, that was what the elders of the village claimed.

The entire region was covered in deep snow. Anyone who had not laid in an adequate amount of supplies went hungry. The snow piled up in gigantic heaps outside the doors of the small houses, thus imprisoning the residents indoors.

The storm caught Viulo Gohan, the old forest-keeper, in his hut in the forest. Two weeks later, when the weather began to improve, the inhabitants of the village arrived and rescued him. He was in a serious condition. After fighting for his life for 30 days, he died, and was buried in the local cemetery.

Grisha Valodiev came to Israel with his parents in 1959. He was born in the Ukraine to a Russian mother, but thanks to his father's dual citizenship, the family managed to immigrate to Israel. They were given a small two-room apartment in a suburb of Haifa. Although Grisha was only 10, a relatively young child, he never felt at home or settled down in Israel. He was a dark boy with curly hair who did not fit in with the blond, blue-eyed Russian immigrant children. On the other hand, his heavy accent made him a misfit among the Israelis as well. Grisha used brute force to make a place for himself on the social ladder. Violence and beatings were routine events. At age 14, he was expelled from school for the last time. His desperate parents did not know what to do with him. Grisha found himself an occupation: he would spend days and nights at the port, inhaling the smells of the ocean, watching the huge ships, and dreaming about the distant lands to which they sailed.

He didn't know when the idea first popped into his head. He simply made a decision and implemented it. He went home, threw a few clothes, personal items and food into a small bag and left a letter of farewell for his parents. One rainy winter morning in 1964, Grisha sneaked into the big hold in the bowels of the cargo ship *Kionoya*. The food he had packed in his bag lasted him for a week. Only then, when he thought that the ship was sufficiently far out at sea, did he go out on deck. Captain Afesko listened to the boy's story for a whole hour. He sucked on his pipe noisily and then said: "If you want, you can stay."

Grisha worked on the cargo ship for seven whole years, in close contact with Captain Afesko. When the High Holydays approached, he would write to his parents to let them know that he was fine. They became accustomed to receiving a letter bearing a colorful stamp from a different country each year. For them, the main thing was that Grisha was alive and happy.

When the time came for Captain Afesko to retire, he suggested that Grisha join him. Grisha accepted the offer gladly. Over the years, Afesko had become his father and spiritual guide, and Grisha loved him dearly. They arrived in Tampere, Finland, on a cold snowy winter day. Afesko's family welcomed Grisha enthusiastically. Tall, dark and handsome, not to mention fluent in Finnish, he became the attraction of the entire village within a few days. It didn't take long for a love affair between Grisha and Johanna, Afesko's 17-year-old daughter, to begin. One day, in their search for a place where they could be alone, they went into the forest. Grisha held Johanna's hand tightly. His whole body began to tremble and he became pale. He led her through the trees until they reached the hut in which Viulo Gohan lay dying some 200 years ago.

Grisha's heart pounded wildly when they climbed up the ladder into the hut at the top of the tree. Despite the ravages of time that were evident, the wooden hut was still in its place. Nobody had been there since the frozen body of the old forest-keeper had been taken down.

For years, Grisha tried to explain what happened in the hut the day he reached it. He had marched deliberately up to the wooden wall on the south side, as if he knew in advance what to do. He counted eight beams from the corner and pulled the beam with all his might. Behind the loose beam, among the spider webs, there was a thick gold ring engraved with two letters: G.V. This was the ring that the forest-keeper's poor relatives had sought for generations and not found.

How did Grisha Valodiev know where the ring was? There can only be one explanation.

The British author and satirist, Samuel Butler (1835-1902), who did not particularly accept the karmic view, nevertheless subscribed to the notion of reincarnation:

We commonly know that we are going to die, though we do not know that we are going to be born. But are we sure this is so? We may have had the most gloomy forebodings on this head and forgotten all about them. ...

I must have it that neither are the good rewarded nor the bad punished in a future state, but every one must start anew quite irrespective of anything they have done here and must try his luck again and go on trying it again and again *ad infinitum*. Some of our lives, then, will be lucky and some unlucky and it will resolve itself into one long eternal life during which we shall change so much that we shall not remember our antecedents very far back (any more than we remember having been embryos) nor foresee our future very much, and during which we shall have our ups and downs *ad infinitum* – effecting a transformation scene at once as soon as circumstances become unbearable.

S. Butler, *The Note-Books of Samuel Butler*

An explanation of the living and the dead spirits

Swami Bakta Vishta

Every spirit of thought, from the spirit of the individual to the spirit of the times, has a beginning, a period of time during which it is built, a period of time during which it is at its peak, and an end. Between the beginning and the end, its actions are controlled by the universal law of cyclicality. The duration of the cycles depends on the consolidation of the thoughts, which creates and nourishes the spirit. When the last cycle occurs, the spirit has ceased to exist.

The spirit of the living person – the physical spirit, the spirit of will and the spirit of thought – may consist of various stages and qualities. The physical spirit is the semi-physical astral form, which binds the cells and the physical matter – called the physical body – in place. The spirit of will is a form that emerges in certain conditions by means of a certain part of the cosmic will, which receives the character of the person and is adapted accordingly. A living person's spirit of thought is what is created in the mental world by means of a continuous action of his consciousness in one direction.

Physical spirits of dead people

There are three types of spirits of dead people: the physical spirit, the spirit of will and the spirit of thought, and there are three combinations of the three. The physical spirit, the spirit of will and the spirit of thought are parts of living people who separate from them with the death of the physical body. The three spirits go on to their worlds, where they stay for some time.

Subsequently, they divide up, disperse, vanish and enter animal forms, but in time, they will get together again and will be used for building the personalities of other people in whom the soul will incarnate when it returns to the earth.

The physical spirit is the basis in which the astral body, or the astral form, is anchored. The astral body becomes a physical spirit after death.

While it is still in the physical body, or when it is leaving it, the form or the physical spirit looks like smoke or like the gas of carbonic acid. It is grayish , reddish, yellowish, bluish or silvery-purple in color. Tne physical body is heavy, but has a low density, while the physical spirit is light, but much denser than the physical body. It weighs between 30 and 120 grams.

The process of dying begins when the bonds of the physical spirit are released from the cells, the organic centers and the nerve centers of the physical body. The process commences in the feet and continues upward. The moment the spirit leaves a certain part of the body, that part becomes cold and devoid of sensation. The astral body curls and rolls upward like smoke until it reaches the heart, where it is reduced to a spherical mass. The heart contracts and the throat swallows, and the spherical mass rises up and leaves through the mouth. Usually, this is how we die; that is the usual exit aperture from the body. However, there are other exit apertures.

It is possible that even though the astral body is now outside the body, death has not yet occurred. The spherical mass may well remain above the physical body for some time, or it may immediately assume a physical form. It can still be linked to the physical body by means of the magnetic thread of life. Death does not occur until the magnetic thread is cut.

The magnetic thread of life consists of four strands that are wound in three sheaths. The prophet sees it as a silvery thread or a fine thread of smoke linking the physical body and the form above it. So long as the thread is not cut, it is possible to revive the body. The moment the thread is cut, death occurs, and neither the astral form nor the physical spirit can revive the physical body.

The spirit of thought and the spirit of will can separate from the physical body only at the time of death, and from each other immediately after death has occurred. They can also remain with the physical spirit for some time. Alternatively, the spirit of will can remain with the physical spirit, and the spirit of thought can separate from both of them. What happens is determined by and depends on what the person thought and did during the life of his physical body. After death, nothing occurs to direct these things.

The state of the physical spirit after death – particularly the state of the spirit of will and the spirit of thought – is determined by the industriousness or idleness of the consciousness and of the will, by the implementation of the knowledge the person had at his disposal or his negligence in implementing it, and by motives that affected the person's thoughts and deeds during his physical life.

It is easy to differentiate between the physical spirit of the dead and the spirit of living people. The physical spirit of the dead person has no life, and it wanders around without any particular goal or purpose. When the physical body disintegrates, the physical spirit loses its consolidated form. When the physical form begins to disintegrate, the physical spirit holds on to it or moves around it like a phosphorescent substance that looks like the moisture of a crumbling log in the dark, and the physical spirit disappears with the body in the same way as the phosphorescent substance disappears when the log turns into dust.

The appearance of physical spirits is controlled by the law of nature, just like everything else. For every living physical thing, there is a body-form, inside it and around it. The physical body is composed of physical matter. The form of the physical body is composed of lunar matter from the moon, about which the average person knows very little. In fact, the physical and lunar matter are similar in nature.

The difference between them lies in the fact that the particles of lunar matter are finer and nearer to one another than those of the physical matter, as well as in the fact that the lunar and physical matter serve as opposing magnetic poles for each other.

The moon is a magnet, and the earth is another magnet. At certain times, the force of gravity of the earth is greater than that of the moon, and at others, the force of gravity of the moon is greater than that of the earth. These times are fixed and regular, and these magnetic attractions, which occur alternately, cause the endless cyclicality of the lunar and physical matter, as well as the phenomenon that is called life and death. What changes in the cyclicality of the lunar and physical matter are the units of life that come from the sun. In order to receive the units of life from the sun that are transferred into a physical structure by means of the lunar matter, a physical body must be created.

After death, the lunar matter returns the units of life to the sun.

Every living thing is affected by the magnetic force of gravity of the moon and the earth. The earth attracts the physical body, and the moon attracts the form that is inside the physical body.

When the earth's force of gravity is stronger than the moon's, the physical spirit is attracted to the physical body that is found under the earth or in the grave, and only rarely is it possible to see it by means of physical sight alone. When the moon's force of gravity is stronger than the earth's, the physical spirit will leave the physical body behind it. The pulse movements or the wavy movements of the physical spirit generally stem from the magnetic action of the earth and the moon. Because of this magnetic action, the spirit will generally be seen a little above or below – usually above – the physical body.

When a spirit moves, it does not walk as if it were on solid ground. The moon's force of gravity is stronger when it is at the peak of its brightness. That is the time in which the probability of the appearance of physical spirits is highest. However, on a brightly moonlit night, it is almost certain that they will not be seen by untrained eyes, since their color is very similar to that of moonlight. It is very easy to discern them in the shadow of a tree, or in a room.

In the epilogue to his play, *Saint* Joan, George Bernard Shaw, the Irish playwright, novelist and critic, has the protagonist emit an anguished cry against reincarnation:

Joan: And now tell me: shall I rise from the dead, and come back to you a living woman? ... What! Must I burn again? Are none of you ready to receive me? ... O God that madest this beautiful earth, when will it be ready to receive Thy saints? How long, O lord, how long?

J. B. Shaw, *Saint Joan*

The German composer, Gustav Mahler was a firm believer in reincarnation. He explained to his friend and biographer, Richard Specht:

"We all return; it is this certainty that gives meaning to life and it does not make the slightest difference whether or not in a later incarnation we remember the former life. What counts is not the individual and his comfort, but the great aspiration to the perfect and the pure which goes on in each incarnation."

As quoted in Richard Specht, *Gustav Mahler* (1913)

The last battle

On March 7, 1990, Uri Gannot was given a ticket to the United States. It was his 25th birthday, and his parents decided to treat their eldest son to an exciting trip abroad. On that trip, it happened for the first time. He began to suffer from acute anxiety attacks. One day, while he was driving through Massachusetts, he got stuck in the usual afternoon traffic jam. It was hot and humid, and even though the fancy Buick was cooled by the best air-conditioning available, Uri began to perspire. His heart pounded and he felt dizzy. He pulled up at the side of the road, got out, and poured a whole bottle of water (he always kept one in the trunk) over his head. Only then, as the cool water was dripping down his back and chest, wetting his expensive silk shirt, did he feel better. Uri cut his trip short and returned to Italy.

The attacks recurred several times. It happened on the way to a game of tennis, on the road to the Roma, on the way to a movie with friends, and twice more when he was coming home from work. Uri was a partner in a successful computer company. He could afford the best treatment.

Dr. Benny Gross's office was on the tenth floor of a fancy office block. Uri arrived at the first appointment upset and worried. After a meticulous and thorough examination, Dr. Gross reassured him that he didn't have a physical problem. The problem was psychological. Dr. Gross referred Uri to a good friend of his, the psychiatrist Shmuel Baram.

It only took eight sessions for Uri, the son of Iraqi immigrants to Italy, to begin to speak fluent German - the kind that was spoken during World War II. When he was in a hypnotic trance, Uri told about a bloody battle in the city of Arfel in Germany in 1945, a battle in which he was killed. Uri claimed that his name was Philip Holmes at the time.

He (Philip Holmes) was a 19-year-old youngster from Massachusetts, the son of German immigrants. He wanted to live and have a good time, but was conscripted. During his first mission, he found himself running through the streets of a foreign city located at the top of a tall cliff. Suddenly there was a barrage of gunfire from all sides.

On March 7, said Holmes, at exactly 11:30, the attack began. The American soldiers came under heavy fire as they advanced toward a large bridge. On Eisenhower's orders, they were prepared for anything. Suddenly, an order not to blow up the bridge came over the radio. Instead, infantry soldiers were sent to scour the city. It was clear to everyone that the loss of life would be high, but during a war, there is no time to stop and think. Holmes was one of the first to run and cross the bridge. There was a volley of well-aimed sniper fire - and ten young soldiers keeled over in a pool of blood. They were replaced by dozens of others, who occupied the city that day and notched up one of the most impressive victories in history. Philip Holmes's body was returned to his parents. A coffin wrapped in the national flag was lowered into the earth in the military cemetery, and the marble plaque was inscribed with the words: Philip Holmes 7.3.45.

The Lebanese-born American author, Kahlil Gibran (1883-1931), spoke of reincarnation in his work, *The Prophet*:

Brief were my days among you, and briefer still the words I have spoken. But should my voice fade in your ears, and my love vanish in your memory, then I will come again, and with a richer heart and lips more yielding to the spirit will I speak. Yes, I shall return with the tide, and though death may hide me and the greater silence enfold me, yet again will I seek your understanding. ... Know, therefore, that from the greater silence I shall return. ... Forget me not that I shall come back to you. ... A little while, a moment of rest upon the wind, and another woman shall bear me.

Kahlil Gibran, *The Prophet*

The vast universe beyond –
Swami Bakta Vishta

Everyone wants to know why man was created.

Everyone wants to know what is awaiting them after death.

Our Creator planned a path with a clear and defined objective, and there has never been any deviation from the plan since the creation of the earth. The purpose and the objective are revealed to us in the steps that have already been taken. We learn that we are approaching the Creator because of the fact that man always moves along a track that meets up with his Creator. Life is just a dream, as we are told, but that does not mean that this is not reality. The dream cannot exist without the person dreaming it. The person lies down to sleep and dream, wakes up and goes to work, and processes this dream in his innovations and inventions, which advance civilization another step toward the final objective. It is also true that by means of the great and important dreams of earthly existence, it is possible to solve the future and the fate of the world, and determine man's place in the universe.

Man is made of a substance that is scattered untidily on the earth, and he enters the womb of a woman in order to be born. That is the process of life. If the Creator wanted to do that, he could have shaped man out of the soul, and left him alone. If the only aim of the creation was for us to live and die here, there would have been no need for the waste and pain involved in our coming and going. It would have been better to create man as he is in maturity. Just as a person produces a car and fills it with gasoline before starting the engine, so it would only have been necessary to breathe the breath of life into him and send him on his way.

Life would be worthless if it did not have a continuation. This is a fact that affects the continuity of man's belief in religion more than any other. With the person's mental development, the consciousness presents its criteria for understanding all things and for measuring them from the point of view of his existence, and our belief in the next world is shattered or reinforced. Nothing looks real or satisfactory to the human life span. When we acknowledge the fact that we are in a dream state, our perception deepens and we see things as they are.

We discern the harmony between our experience on earth and the reason for the creation.

Life is an ongoing and continuous rebirth.

We advance from birth to birth, from dream to dream. Eventually, we will reach a state of wakefulness: then the true realization of our calling will begin. There has always been a link that connects the present and the past, and there has always been a thread of life that connects us with the past.

Pearl S. Buck (1892-1973), an American author who wrote about the Far East, described her view of reincarnation in her novel, *The Living Reed*:

At first Yul-han thought of the child only as his son, a part of himself, a third with Induk. As time passed, however, a most strange prescience took hold of [Yul-han's] mind and spirit. ... He perceived that the child possessed an old soul. It was not to be put in words, this meaning of an old soul. Yul-han, observing the child, saw in his behaviour a reasonableness, a patience, a comprehension, that was totally unchildlike. He did not scream when his food was delayed, as other infants do. Instead, his eyes calm and contemplative, he seemed to understand and was able to wait. These eyes, quietly alive, moved from Yul-han's face to Induk's when they talked, as though he knew what his parents said. ... He gazed at them with such intelligence, such awareness, that it was as if he spoke their names, not as his parents, but as persons whom he recognized. ... Yul-han, watching, felt a certain awe, a hesitancy in calling him "my son," as though the claim were presumption. "If I were a Buddhist," he told Induk one day, "I would say that this child is an incarnation of some former great soul."

Pearl S. Buck, *The Living Reed* (1963)

Rebirth

Civilized man was the first being created by the Creator that was suitable to be reborn. The forms that preceded him were only milestones.

Is there any proof that man is suitable to be reborn today? Yes. Here it is: The aim of the creation is to create forms from matter. When there was no life on earth, everything, everywhere, was in a state of chaos. There was no life. Matter was controlled by certain laws in preparation for the plant life that appeared later on. Ultimately, more developed forms were created, and in time, thousands of new species and animals. Finally, man – the highest form in the animal kingdom – appeared, followed by civilized man. Only after the appearance of the latter was an effort made to create inanimate forms.

Now, two living and creative processes are at work. They each have a clear mission. The first is the creation of life, and the second is the creation of physical forms. They are both made from the same substance as the earth.

The Creator is the cause of everything. Life and the physical forms are created in accordance with his plan. Man enters into partnership with his Creator. Physical forms are created by the force that is at work through him. That proves that man is the highest form of life in this world.

Man is not perfect, since he has not yet reached absolute wholeness. Now he is advancing slowly. He is in a dream state; and just like in his dreams, everything appears upside-down. With his normal consciousness and his physical body, he can slowly see and feel the real experiences that seem unrealistic to him, while those that are not real seem real to him. That is because his physical brain is not yet able to absorb what is really real. However, we are quickly reaching the stage in which we will acquire the skills to understand what is real. Ultimately, everybody will be born with those powers, and then it will be possible to attain direct friendship with the Creator. The screen that separates us from him will be corroded very thin. In our days, many people have succeeded in penetrating it, which means that it is not elusive. When you reach this stage, your true life will begin.

Remember: You will acquire knowledge about everything in your thoughts. All the facts that are linked to instincts stem from universal thoughts.

All the human experiences and activities of life on earth are linked to our dream life, but they do not provide us with facts that are linked to our instincts, and for that reason, they are not a part of universal thought.

When we reach the real world, there will not be any facts other than those of universal thought. When your consciousness is so developed that you can receive and absorb knowledge from the universal consciousness, you will change amazingly. Then you will hold the key to the other knowledge, and ultimately your highest instinct will develop. You know:

There is life after death.

Life on earth is a dream.

The creation of the form is the purpose of existence.

Man was created in order to create physical forms.

Although man is the highest animal on earth, he is not yet suitable to be an eternal friend of the Creator.

Man can become the partner of the Creator, and he will have the power to create matter from chaos.

Man is quickly advancing to the peak of existence, and he has to take only one more step in order to attain eternal friendship with his Creator. By his own efforts, he must extricate himself from a lack of physical reality to non-physical reality.

Immortality is the final stop for all of us

When the following qualities exist in the person, he is capable of reaching the stage of immortality:

He lives a pure life

He is sincere

He only operates honestly

He lives with a clear goal in front of his eyes.

The goal helps us understand the plan of creation and act accordingly. We see the light and want others to see it, too. According to the law of attraction, like attracts like.

What proof do we have of existence after death?

It is easy to prove that the person's soul leaves his body at the moment of death. It is not possible to see this with normal vision because that is the Creator's plan. He wanted his exit to be an honorable event. For those people who do not know the reasons for the fact that it is well known that there is existence after death, I will present several convincing experiences. These experiences have been investigated thoroughly and meticulously, and there is no doubt as to their veracity.

"Dead people, always in their usual clothes, were seen hovering outside the windows during the day and night."

"Dead people were seen and identified from a great distance, hovering over fields and forests."

"Dead people were seen above our heads, in houses, rooms, the open air, both during the day and during the night."

Many people have had similar experiences to the one below:

Sitting in a room and looking around suddenly, they saw a relative standing in front of them. He disappeared the moment they noticed him. Later, they discovered that the self-same relative had died at the exact moment he had appeared before them. In many cases, they felt certain that something had happened to a particular person. They subsequently discovered that he had been killed or had died at the very moment they had seen him.

What happens at the moment of death?

At the moment of death, the soul leaves the body. With the liberation of the soul, there is no longer any need for physical sleep, and you are completely awake. You still have the intelligence you had in your life, and in most cases, you do not know that you have died. You try to speak, but you cannot. You try to cause other people to see you, but you cannot. You understand that you are powerless, and you do not understand why the people who are looking at you are not seeing you. You still do not understand that you have liberated yourself from your body. You think that there are undoubtedly other people with whom you can talk. You wander to another area, but even so you are unable to speak to the people you know. You can appear at your own funeral without understanding what happened. Then you feel that the power has been taken away from you, and it seems that you do not have control over the end.

In the few cases in which life returned to the body after leaving it, the spirit of life still preserved all of its power.

When we are reborn, we do not remember any experience or sin from the past. If our relatives or friends are with us, we will recognize them and know who we know on earth.

In the new life, we will not recognize anything that is not pleasant. We will not know of the fate of our friends and relatives who may have been condemned to destruction.

We frequently link up to the depths of the sea, and that is the time during which our entire being is filled with a feeling of the divine presence blessing our existence. If you would only succumb to the gentle effects of the visits that take place while you are asleep, you could learn a great deal about life on the other side.

An immortal body

Man's body has been designed so that he can do anything. Here on earth there are creatures that can fly, walk, swim, float or hover; creatures that can move quickly or slowly. None of these can do all of these things at the same time. Each one has its limitations, but all of the powers exist in each one. In the other world, we do not have a physical body because there is no physical matter as we know it. In order for us to understand this better, we must remember that universal thought undergoes a chain of stages and changes in order to create matter from light. The body we have there is not made of chemical elements, as is our body here, but rather from a material that preceded the stage in which those elements appeared. That is the stage of development that preceded the creation of real matter, as we call it, and the giving of shape to that mass. This would imply that creatures regress after death, but that is not the case. It is only the form being liberated from its physical burden and cleansed of the chaos from which it was created. What our eyes perceive as material and real is just a dream – since material is unstable and changeable and breaks down quickly into its components.

The body of the soul is a part of universal thought that has advanced beyond the stage of light, but has not yet reached the stage of the chemical elements.

The law of the good

In certain senses, this is the most wonderful law of all, since it leads from the earth to the blessed life. The law states:

"Every positive impulse and activity of value that has taken root in the world will continue to exist until it bears fruit in the future world."

This law does not relate to a single impulse or to a single action, but rather only to deeds that began to take root for all time. It is worthwhile remembering that. Sudden efforts and regrets on one's deathbed are only of small value. They do not have the power to purchase eternal life.

What is the meaning of infinity?

Everything that continues forever is infinite. Our last place of residence in the future is infinite and the life that exists there is infinite. The place and the life are similar to each other. Here on earth, both life and matter are transitory. Our body, the air and the earth are involved in a process of dissolution. The end of every physical thing is disintegration. Life here, in all of its forms, is transitory.

When death does not exist

When the elements of nature are not used, no change occurs. The infinite soul is not composed of the elements, and therefore it does not change, and nothing can harm it. It is not in danger from enemies since it cannot be attacked, drowned or poisoned; beatings do not hurt it, nor do falls injure it, because there is no element that can harm it. It does not feel fire or lightning.

Life, therefore, continues forever.

Richard Bach (1936-), an American author and aviator, wrote the novel *Jonathan Livingstone Seagull*, in which a seagull incarnates:

"Where is everybody, Sullivan?" he asked silently, quite at home now with the easy telepathy that these gulls used instead of screes and gracks. "Why aren't there more of us here? Why, where I came from there were..."

"...thousands and thousands of gulls, I know." Sullivan shook his head. "The only answer I can see, Jonathan, is that you are pretty well a one-in-a-million bird. Most of us came along ever so slowly. We went from one world into another that was almost exactly like it, forgetting right away where we had come from, not caring where we were headed, living for the moment. Do you have any idea how many lives we must have gone through before we even got the first idea that there is more to life than eating, or fighting, or power in the Flock? A thousand lives, Jon, ten thousand! And then another hundred lives until we began to learn that there is such a thing as perfection, and another hundred again to get the idea that our purpose for living is to find that perfection and show it forth. The same rule holds for us now, of course; we choose our next world through what we learn in this one. Learn nothing, and the next world is the same as this one, all the same limitations and lead weights to overcome. ... But you, Jon, learned so much at one time that you didn't have to go through a thousand lives to reach this one."

Richard Bach, *Jonathan Livingstone Seagull* (1970)

Vikings discover a world

Vivian Branson was an ordinary English girl, with a fair complexion, blonde hair and blue eyes. What made her special was her height. Not every girl can boast a height of five foot eleven. More than once, people told her that she looked like a Viking, but Vivian did not give it a second thought.

At age 19, after a short secretarial course, she got a job in a large real estate company in central London. Every day, on her way home from the office, she would stop in the neighborhood pub. She always ordered the same drink - a double whiskey with ice. One day, she noticed an older man sitting at the bar. He reminded her of the actor, Omar Shariff, in old movies she had seen long ago. She was not surprised when he offered to buy her a drink. The conversation between them flowed easily. He told her that his name was John McJefferson. He was a Scottish psychiatrist who had come to a professional congress in London for ten days. The two of them met unexpectedly in the pub the next day, too. Their third meeting was arranged.

On their fourth meeting, Vivian invited John home, and he was surprised to see the paintings that covered the walls of her small apartment. She told him that lately she had been painting almost every evening. He told her that he was closely acquainted with the place that kept recurring in her works. He pulled a pendulum out of the inside pocket of his woolen jacket. It was a transparent stone hanging on a long chain. Within a few minutes, Vivian had gone into a hypnotic trance.

She described an ancient period when she had been a young man called Sopan on a Viking ship that was headed for the Scottish island of Inchmarnock in southwest Scotland. Sopan told about the difficult weeks at sea and the bitter battle that took place when they finally disembarked on the island.

The seafarers clashed with the the Scots!, single-minded people who fought for everything on their land. Sopan was only 16 when he bled to death on the battlefield covered with wildflowers. He lay there with many of his companions and waited for death to liberate him from his agony. And then the vultures descended... Vivian woke up from the hypnotic trance she had been in for an hour. Even John Majefferson, with his extensive experience, was surprised at the typical 11th-century Viking dialect spoken in a young man's voice by a London girl who had never left her native city. During their next meeting, Vivian continued talking about long-ago experiences on the island of Inchmarnock. It looked as if she had returned to the place over and over again. Besides being Sopan, the Viking youth, it turned out that Vivian had been on the island during the time of the Christian saint, Murnock. The latter even built a monastery there, and Vivian drew a detailed and accurate sketch of the plan of the monastery. Her sketch was later validated.

John Majefferson recorded and took down everything Vivian had said under hypnosis. Subsequently, when he played the recording to her, she herself found it difficult to identify her voice, let alone understand the things that had been said in a language with which she was unfamiliar.

Ronnie - Sami

Kaufinan had lived in Lapland all his life. The region where he lived was near the town of Lito, somewhere between Sweden and Norway. That morning, he got up particularly early in order to go to the market. He harnessed the dogs to the big sleigh that was loaded with furs, jams and beads. Snow was falling as Kaufinan set out. His mother waved goodbye to him from the opening of the *kuta*, small tent in which they lived. That was the last time anyone saw him...

Near the end of his military service in the paratrooper division, Ronnie suddenly experienced an acute lack of peace of mind. His final three months of service passed annoyingly slowly. The day after his discharge, Ronnie went into the travel agency that was nearest to his parents' home. "I want to go to the furthest and coldest place possible," he told the young smiling travel agent.

A few days later, Ronnie was on a plane to Scandinavia. His first stop was a small town called Ivlu on the shores of the frozen Inari lake. Ronnie arrived there on a Thursday, the day when the local market was swarming with people. Only after an hour did Ronnie realize that he actually understood bits of sentences. He was very surprised at this. The local Lapps, who were called Sami, spoke a strange language that was different than anything he had every heard. Ronnie continued wandering around the market, enchanted by the sights, colors, smells and cleanliness. In his childhood he was accustomed to different scenes. Here everything was quiet. The stalls were tidy and the agricultural produce was arranged in neat piles on the wooden counters, like rows of soldiers.

Ronnie met Lassa, who would later become his best friend, on his second day in the market. Lassa spoke a little English, so they could communicate. When Lassa invited Ronnie to his home, the latter had no reason to think twice. The small wooden house was simply furnished, and Lassa's parents and sister extended Ronnie a warm welcome. The next morning, they awoke to a snowstorm and stayed in the house all day, drinking hot tea and eating vegetable soup. It was two days until they could go out again. They passed the time telling stories about local life and asking Ronnie about his country of origin and his family. Ronnie got into the work of branding the family herd surprisingly quickly. The letter R - the first letter of his hosts' surname, Robnaymi - was branded on to the hindquarters of the unfortunate animals. Their skin burned while their feet were covered by the cold snow.

Only after four more days of work did Ronnie suddenly realize that he was branding the animals with the first letter of his name. Coincidence? He chuckled to himself quietly. A herd of deer and gazelles may be something special here in distant Lapland, but it was doubtful that it would impress anyone at home.

Six months passed. Ronnie became a member of his adoptive family's household. He felt comfortable in the faraway land, among the endless snowfields, the foaming rivers and the forests. The thing he loved the most was eating the smoked fish they prepared by themselves, and the soup Lassa's mother made.

In time, Ronnie began to earn a living as a rafting instructor on the Kami-Juki River for tourists in search of adventure. He continued visiting the market at least twice a week, and on other days transported merchandise on his snow-cycle in order to help Fiona, his blue-eyed fiancée. One thing he was not prepared to do, and that was to get on to a sleigh drawn by dogs... When Lassa tried to convince him to do so a few times, Ronnie stubbornly refused.

One evening, when everyone was sitting around the table in Lassa's home, Ronnie told them for the umpteenth time about his home and the country he came from, where the soil was yellow and sandy, and there was never any snow. At a certain point in the evening, Ela, Lassa's mother, took out a carefully folded colored handkerchief containing small dry wooden sticks. She spread them out on the handkerchief and Lassa explained that she wanted to ask the great spirits how it had happened that of all the people in the area, Ronnie had come to their house.

Ela rubbed the sticks between her hands and threw them on to the table. What she saw made her turn pale. She remained silent for a long time, and then she whispered: "Your grandmother, Lassa, claims that Ronnie was the son she lost before I was born. One morning he went to the market on a sleigh with dogs and never returned. Now I understand everything..."

The Skeleton Coast

On January 18, 1990, a cold and rainy winter's day, seven people got into an SAA plane. Their objective was a trip to Namibia. The initiator of the idea was Bella Hodorov, a 36-year-old single biologist who had collected a group of aficionados of the desert and adventure.

It all began during Bella's studies, when she read about the Vellozia plant that grew in Namibia. The plant produces one pair of leaves only, but these leaves sometimes reach a length of three yards. These special plants can survive for 1,000 years - some botanists claim that they can even live for 2,000 years!

Bella felt that she had to see this marvelous plant growing in its natural habitat. She began to sound out the idea with some of her friends. By the end of the year, a group of four men and three women had formed with the intention of going way down south: Gershon the archeologist, Doron the photographer, Ronnie the biologist, and Moshe the advertising exec. Besides Bella, there were two other women - Miriam the travel agent and Dalia the anthropologist.

On that cold and rainy January day, when they left Ben-Gurion Airport, Bella didn't know that she was going on the biggest adventure of her life.

The first stop was Cape Cross. Bella knew that that was the

place where the Portuguese explorer Diego Cad, had walked 500 years previously. What seemed strange was that it was so familiar to her. After the group had marveled at the masses of seals that inhabited the region, they continued northward toward the Skeleton Coast. This strip of coastline is world-famous because of the hundreds of ships that ran aground there; their wrecks can be seen to this day.

The next day, everyone went on a jeep tour in the famous dunes. Bella, however, preferred to go off on her own. As far as she knew, the place was a unique nature reserve. In the morning, she wandered around the Damarland region, where it is easy to get lost. After taking a break for lunch, she went down to the shore. Behind one of the gigantic rocks, she saw a pile of rusty iron bars. There wasn't a whole lot left of what had once been a ship. Bella sat on the soft sand and stared at the clean blue water, trying to imagine the human tragedy that had occurred there once, when a ship, full of emigrants with high hopes of easy riches, had foundered on the rocks.

Bella awoke with a start: it was dusk, almost completely dark. She realized that she had fallen asleep. The impression of the dream she had had was still fresh - so much so that she found it difficult to differentiate between imagination and reality. Bella remembered the scene clearly: She saw herself wearing a long dress and a hat with a feather, sitting beside a large table covered with a white tablecloth, laden with an abundance of delicacies in white dishes decorated with golden flowers. There were many people sitting around the large table, and she recognized several familiar faces among them. They were all on the way to Namibia, to the place where, they had been told, there were diamonds in the sand. Suddenly there was a tremendous noise, and the ship listed sideways. Someone screamed. Then, all hell broke loose. It was every man for himself. Bella ran to the cabin where her one-year-old son, Hans, was asleep with her husband, Theodore, but the cabin was empty. Apparently they had already gotten into one of the lifeboats. Bella rushed up to the deck. She was pushed aside roughly by a fat man who was hurrying to get into the lifeboat. Bella fell into the stormy waters...

Darkness fell on everything. Bella sat stunned on the soft sand. She knew - simply knew - the explanation for the dream she had dreamed. She had been here in the past, drowned off these shores, and returned in order to experience closure. Everything was suddenly so clear. Even after 300 years, Bella could feel the pain of separation from her husband, her son and the life she knew then. Tears flowed from her eyes and she didn't even bother to wipe them. All she wanted was a small sign - something that could prove that it wasn't just a dream.

Later on that evening, when Bella went to the local pub with her friends, she met a man who had come on a visit to his former homeland from London, where he was now living.

"Hi, I'm Theodore," he said. "Haven't I seen you somewhere before?"

Three fingers

Robert Nelson was one of the hundreds of passengers who got off the plane in Papua. It was afternoon, and deep down inside, Robert marveled at the fact that it was possible to go from the orderly streets of Melbourne, Australia, where he lived, into the primitive world within few hours.

Robert had not planned to come here. For 22 years, he had worked in a computer-programming company. He was a middle-aged man with a large paunch and thick glasses, who spent most of his time in front of the computer in his office. He had never been very successful with women, both because of his appearance and because of his withdrawn nature. What had bothered him in the past had gradually become a habit. He loved solitude.

And then the offer came. The general manager of the company invited him to a meeting in his comfortable office on the 17th floor of the building. There, without preamble, he offered him a particularly tempting contract, on condition that he establish a new branch in Papua. Robert Nelson burst out laughing. He really thought that it was a good joke. To choose him, of all people - the biggest square and stick-in-the-mud... However, as the conversation progressed, he found himself listening attentively. Two hours later, they had signed the necessary agreements. Robert Nelson went home and began to pack.

The day he arrived in Papua, the fingers of his right hand began to hurt. For three days he was busy settling into the small apartment he had at his disposal. On the fourth day, instead of going to the office and starting to work, he went to a doctor. A lengthy series of tests revealed nothing. Pills, X-rays - he tried everything, but to no avail. Robert returned to the office. He began to brief the three local workers who were supposed to serve as the mainstays of the local company.

Spike, a local resident and colleague, noticed Robert's sore and distorted fingers. He cautiously suggested that they visit the chief - the local regional doctor of the Holi tribe. Robert scornfully rejected the suggestion, but after three more days of acute pain, found himself begging Spike to take him. After a half-hour ride, they reached the chief's house. The man, who was dark-skinned with long frizzy hair, wore a garment made of leather and feathers. He took the two men to a cave in the mountain. There were large black stones scattered at the entrance. Inside the cave, on improvised shelves of clean tree-trunks, there were painted skulls standing in straight rows.

Robert, Spike and the chief sat on the ground around a fire. Robert drank water from a clay bowl. Spike explained that it was simply water in which juniper leaves had been soaking. The beverage was warm and strong. During the conversation, which Spike translated, Robert became dizzy from the odor of the leaves that were burning in the smoke of the fire. He repeated aloud the incomprehensible words uttered by the chief. Afterwards, darkness enveloped everything.

When Robert awoke from the deep sleep he had fallen into,

he saw the chief and Spike looking at him affectionately. They gave him a hot drink that he didn't recognize. While he was drinking, Spike played a recording of the conversation he had recorded on the small executive tape recorder Robert had given him on the first day of work.

Robert recognized his own voice even though he didn't understand a word he was saying. What sounded like gibberish was, it transpired, a dialect of one of the 800 languages spoken in the region. "I was here 119 years ago. My name was Mankan..." When her husband and two sons had died in a battle with the neighboring tribe, she had cut off three fingers of her right hand, which was the conventional sign of mourning...

Robert listened to the translation and the explanations in silence. He maintained his silence even when the chief poured the blood of a large lizard into the fire, with the help of a long feather. After another hour of sitting in the smoke that rose from the fire, Robert got up to go home. Although he felt slightly dizzy, it was obvious beyond a shadow of a doubt that the pain in his right hand had disappeared.

Pearls and champagne

The lawyer, Dror Golan, stood quiet and pale. The doctor at the pathological institute rolled back the white sheet covering the body, and all at once he saw the face of his wife, Sharon. Despite her death pallor, she was as beautiful as ever. Dror nodded and bent over to kiss her dead face. Deep in his heart, he wondered how Sharon's hair still exuded the fragrance he loved so much. He straightened, looked at the face he had loved for thirty years, and went out. In his shaking hands, he was holding the small polyethylene bag containing the pearl earrings and the chain the doctor had handed him.

That is how Sharon's body had been found - elegantly dressed, down to the last detail, including the expensive jewelry. She died in the same way as she lived - like a true lady.

Dror called his parents from a call-box and asked them to go to his house and wait for his son, Shai, when he came home from school. He himself hurried to make all the necessary arrangements for the funeral.

Dror wondered where Sharon had gotten hold of the sleeping pills she had swallowed. He suspected that Dr. Ami Strauss, Sharon's childhood friend, had had a hand in it. On at least two different occasions, Sharon had told Dror that Ami had promised not to let her suffer too much. When she was informed that the cancer had spread to her liver and spine, she knew that it was only a matter of time. The pain increased, and the treatments could do nothing but postpone the inevitable end. After a certain period of time, she gave up chemotherapy and made do with pain-killers.

Sharon planned everything. She even left a letter, which Dror found in their safety-deposit box in the bank a month after her death. "I wanted you to remember me always beautiful, fragrant and laughing, like I was before I got ill. Forgive me for leaving. I'll always love you. Yours, Idit." Dror didn't understand why Sharon had signed the name Idit. It was her middle name in her ID card, but she never used it.

Twenty years passed. Shai, now 26 years old, returned from a trip to the Far East. A week later, Dror opened his son's bedroom door to find a lovely young girl standing in the middle of the room, clad only in her bra and pants. Surprised, he shut the door...

At breakfast, everyone made an effort to remain polite and serious. Shai introduced his girlfriend, Idit, and announced that they were about to get married. After that morning, Dror met Idit's parents and family several times. Three months later, family and friends gathered in the garden in order to celebrate Shai and Idit's wedding.

When the wedding photographs arrived, Dror was sitting alone on the terrace, looking out at the hill opposite and remembering his and Sharon's wedding so many years ago. He was overcome with a wave of nostalgia and he went over to the crowded bookshelf and took out an album in which he kept all the old pictures.

Only when he took out their wedding picture and placed it on the glass table did he realize that there was a surprising resemblance between the two women. He was amazed that he had not noticed it until that day.

During the next visit, Dror retrieved Sharon's pearls and earrings from the safe and gave them to Idit with tears in his eyes. "I feel that these jewels are yours," he said in a trembling voice...

Dinner in Paris

Fifty-two-year-old David Ga'aton was known as a successful and shrewd businessman among his friends. He was the man who built the large, fancy swimming-pools for the country's wealthy. He was the one to whom people turned when they wanted an architectural dream realized. David specialized in turning his clients' whims into reality. Of course, everything was a matter of price. For 15 years since his discharge from the army, David had been making a lot of money. Three and a half years ago, he had built a large, elegant villa in a prestigious neighborhood in Ramat Hasharon, one of Israel's wealthier cities. He had everything: a lovely wife, two successful children and a flourishing career. At least twice a year, he and Yafit would travel abroad. He would attend professional fairs and order the latest samples of tiles and related materials. Yafit would go shopping and meet him for dinner. David was always the first to introduce all the latest and the most breathtaking innovations into Israel. Every now and then, he would also go to the Far East. He preferred to go there alone and mix business with pleasure. What Yafit didn't know wouldn't hurt her - that's how he salved his conscience...

In 1993, because of the economic slump, David found himself caught in a severe recession. He would sit in his fancy office for hours, waiting for the fax machine to announce his salvation.

However, as if to annoy him deliberately, the fax machine remained silent.

No matter what he did or tried, it simply didn't work. The flow of opportunities had dried up. His turnover decreased to almost nothing, but his expenses remained high. The limited savings of the Ga'aton family were used up. At the end of the High Holyday season, David felt that he had reached the end of his tether. Yafit did not stop nagging him during long conversations that continued deep into the night, and he didn't know what to answer her. He decided not to wait for everything to collapse, so he went to his usual travel agency and ordered one ticket to Paris.

A light rain was falling when the plane landed at Orly Airport. David hurried from the terminal and flagged down the first cab he saw. He was tired and wanted to get to his hotel as quickly as possible. It was six o'clock in the evening, and he thought to himself with satisfaction that so far, everything was going according to the schedule he had set. Dinner, a shower and a good night's sleep. The next morning, he had other plans: a lot of phone calls and meetings. David relaxed in the back seat and dozed off to the sounds of soft music coming from the cab's tape deck.

David woke up in a panic. He glanced at his watch and was astounded to see that the hands indicated eight thirty. "There are traffic jams, Monsieur, because of the rain," said the driver. He leaned forward and saw the lovely young face of a girl with her hair neatly tied back beneath a black beret. "You're a girl," he mumbled in embarrassment. "Yes," she answered, "Is that a problem?" They both burst out laughing. Monique, the driver, introduced herself formally. She told David that she was a 25-year-old law student who was paying her way through school by working as a cab driver. Both her parents had been killed when she was only seven, she explained. Since then she had been brought up in the home of her elderly grandparents. He found himself telling her about his troubles at home and in the business. At a certain point, she turned to him again and suggested that they stop and have a drink at one of the restaurants along the freeway. David suddenly realized how hungry he was; anyway, the traffic wasn't moving, and he thought to himself that he wasn't in that much of a hurry. They stopped at the Motel Bordeau at the first opportunity they had to get off the freeway. It was a lovely old building in the shape of a horseshoe in the middle of which there was a restaurant with large wooden windows. The parking lot boasted a small fountain that looked rather funny in the middle of the pouring rain. David and Monique entered the restaurant dripping and laughing. They sat down at a small table covered with a red-and-white checkered tablecloth. They ordered steak and potatoes and a bottle of red wine. Two hours later, after a second bottle of wine had been consumed, it was clear to both of them that neither of them was going anywhere that night. The pouring rain and the wind, along with the intimacy and closeness growing between them, left no room for doubt about the rest of the evening. They registered at reception, took a key and went up to a room on the second floor. David remembered that night for a long time afterwards.

The week he spent in Paris was a medley of passionate romantic encounters and futile business meetings. Monique and David did not speak much after that first evening of getting acquainted. Their passion and their sensual intoxication overpowered them, and they preferred to spend every free moment in bed. They went back over and over again to the motel where they had spent the first evening. Everything was so familiar and comfortable, just like being at home. On the last day of David's stay in Paris, Monique took him to the house in which she had grown up. Next to the river stood a very old house with two enormous oak trees standing beside it. David caught his breath. The house was very familiar to him, as if he had been there before. Even before he had passed over the threshold, he already knew how everything would look inside. When they went into the comfortable living-room, which was furnished with antiques, he insisted for some reason on going over to the large fireplace and touching the red bricks surrounding it. "Once there was an opening here," he said to himself. "A door, stairs or small tunnel. Perhaps someone hid a treasure here," he joked, noticing the astonished looks of the owners... Monique's grandparents laughed politely. "The house has belonged to the family for 500 years, but we don't know anything about a flight of stairs on this side."

At the end of the week, David returned to Israel, but nothing was the same as before. Monique was not just a passing affair. He dreamed about her at night - her long, straight, brown hair, her big eyes looking at him while they were making love, the old house in the village, and a long, narrow flight of stairs that led to a tunnel outside the village. She neither wrote nor called. However, he kept her address well hidden among his papers. He felt that he had to return to her, but how could he leave his wife and children?

Three months of nightmare-haunted nights passed. One fateful Friday, David closed the office early. After all, he wasn't busy. He had made an appointment with a renowned fortune-teller who had been recommended to him by a client. When they had spoken about it at the time, David had laughed and declared that he didn't believe in "things like that". Now that he was in distress, however, he decided to give it a try.

David reached the address the woman had given him over the phone. He entered a small, crowded apartment. On a faded floral sofa sat an elderly woman wearing a black dress. He sat down opposite her, and when she raised her eyes, he saw a penetrating blue gaze, the likes of which he had never seen. Somehow, he felt that he had come to the right place. Simona the witch, as he called her secretly, knew a lot of personal details about him. She told him about the accident he'd had at age nine, when a miracle had saved him, about an incident in the army when he had almost been taken prisoner, and about the two children who had been born to him over the years. Suddenly she turned pale and her tone of voice changed, becoming aggressive:

"You already left her once a long time ago. Don't do it again. You lived with her in the big stone house at the top of the hill next to the river, and during the Black Plague she took care of you, but that was your time to go. After you died, she fled with the children out of the village, through the tunnel you dug inside the house. She's waiting. Now you have an opportunity to pay your debt..."

The market in Morocco

Rebecca Klaus always knew that she would get to Morocco. For several years, since she began to take an interest in mysticism and meditation, she knew that she belonged there. Often, when her spirit hovered in another place, she saw herself dressed as a belly dancer, in sparkling clothes, gyrating on the yellow desert sands. Opposite, there was a group of dark-skinned men watching her with hungry eyes. At the end of the dance, when she was drenched in perspiration and trembling with the effort, a tall man with green eyes approached her. He gently led her to the far end of a large tent, bent down, and placed heavy iron shackles around her ankles. She didn't understand the language he was speaking, but his eyes said everything. He would return later at night and bring her leftovers from the men's meal. There, on the mat, far from the rest of the girls, she would fall fast asleep. This continued until the day they reached the big city. There the wealthy men of the town who had come to purchase lovely young slaves were waiting for them.

The air was hot and sticky, and the odor of unfamiliar spices enveloped Rebecca Klaus the moment she disembarked from the plane. Her white silk shirt stuck to her perspiring body, even though it was late at night. At home, in Belgium, it was winter, and she had stuffed the thick coat into a large carry-on bag she had prepared earlier.

The cab driver took Rebecca to the Tishaka Hotel, not far from the city of Marrakesh. The hotel was luxurious and decorated with carved tablets of stone in the local style. At the side of the hotel, between lawns and palm trees, she relaxed beside a large swimming-pool, which was completely lined with blue mosaic. Near the pool stood a small building that resembled a mosque, whose rounded ceiling was decorated with colorful stars and various geometric shapes. Rebecca fell in love with the place instantly. Everything enchanted her. She felt like a little girl who had gone into a fairy-tale...

The Jewish religion

Some religious Jews vehemently reject the notion of reincarnation. They also deny the existence of this idea among the ancient Jewish philosophies. On the other hand, there are rabbis who view this phenomenon as an inseparable part of Judaism.

Shlomo Asch mentions in one of his books: "Not the power to remember but rather the power to forget is a prerequisite for our existence." If the notion of reincarnation is correct, it means that during the intermediary phase, when the soul switches from one body to the next, it has to go through the sea of oblivion.

Sometimes, the angel in charge of the process of oblivion, which is so vital, "forgets" to do his work. We remember bits of information from the previous world in which we lived, and this causes us to be haunted by memories from other lives. These memories sweep like clouds from a mountain-peak into the valley of thought, and interweave themselves into the events of our lives. They manifest themselves in nightmares. Sometimes a person hears voices from another dimension.

In the first century CE, the Jewish historian, Josephus Flavius, discussed the topic of reincarnation in his book, *The Wars of the Jews*. In the capacity of his position as a general in the army that fought the Romans, he was among the few who survived the bloody battle. He was deeply affected by the soldiers who intended to take their own lives rather than fall into captivity: "People's bodies are indeed human and meant for destruction. However, the soul is eternal, and it is the eternal part that enters our body. Do you not know that anyone who leaves this life in a natural way gains eternal life and glory? ... In the eternal development, they are sent into the pure fields again ... and those who act in madness against themselves are received in the dark place that belongs to the god of death, Hades."

Josephus also explained how various streams in Judaism relate to the issue of reincarnation. Some people related to the body literally, and in their opinion, the soul died along with the body. Others claimed that only the souls of good people remained. Such a soul leaves the dead body and passes on to another body, while the souls of the wicked are condemned to unending punishment.

The Essenes left us the Dead Sea Scrolls in which they described their religious beliefs, among other things. They believed that the soul survives physical death. Even though it is not mentioned specifically, it is known that the Essenes based their beliefs on the notion of reincarnation that was later transferred to the theory of Kabbalah.

An important figure at the time was the Alexandrian philosopher Guadius. In his treatise, *De Sumnis*, he said: "The air is full of souls. The ones that are near to the earth come down in order to join up with human bodies."

In another place, he wrote: "The company of souls that lack a body constitutes a disruptive element... Some of the souls are meant to enter a human body, and, after a predetermined period of time, leave it for freedom... Souls that reach a high sacred level are liberated from the bonds that bind them to the earth. Souls come down to earth in order to learn and acquire knowledge."

Rabbi Moshe Gaster relates to the notion of reincarnation in his writings that appear in *The Encyclopedia of Religions and Peoples*. He wrote: "There is no doubt that this idea is very ancient in Judaism. The Samaritans, in their sacred writings, related to the idea of the existence of a soul that was given to the first man, and went through the incarnations to Seth, to Noah, to Abraham, and afterwards to Moses."

In Judaism, there are no detailed explanations concerning reincarnation, but in other places, it is mentioned as an idea that is self-evident.

In the Kabbalah, it is mentioned that King David was an incarnation of the first man, and he was destined to return one day as the Messiah.

The Kabbalah is supposed to represent the hidden wisdom behind the Bible, and it is the fruit of rabbis from the Middle Ages and perhaps even earlier. The first people to call themselves "kabbalists" were in fact the Tannas [great scholars] who lived in Jerusalem. The central claim states that Moses received both the Law and the wisdom of the Kabbalah [the root of the Hebrew word *Kabbalah* means *to receive*] on Mt. Sinai. The words of the Kabbalah are no less powerful and valid than the commandments on the tablets of the law. There were even people who claimed that the Kabbalah is "above the law".

Pico della Mirandola, the Italian humanist and kabbalist, explained that the great spiritual teachers such as Moses transmitted their law orally via 70 rabbis, until the words were written down in the books of the Kabbalah.

There were many kabbalists at work during the Middle Ages, among them Rabbi Isaac Luria, who founded a special school in the Galilee. Rabbi Chaim Vitel wrote *The Tree of Life*, and this book in fact served as the basis for the book, *The Beginning of the Wheels,* written by the kabbalist Van Rostenrot (1636-1679). The book explains the development of the soul and the plan according to which the principle of reincarnation operates.

The topic of reincarnation appears in the Talmud as well: God causes the person's soul to incarnate in another body, because the person failed to observe one of the commandments that every Jew has to observe. However, even the father of the prophets, Moses, did not observe all of the commandments. (In the opinion of the kabbalists, the first man sinned, and his soul passed on to David. David sinned and therefore his soul passed on to the Messiah.)

The writings of the Kabbalah are traditionally attributed to Rabbi Simeon Bar Yochai, who fled from Jerusalem and wrote the *Zohar* [*Book of Splendor*] in hiding. After his death, two of his pupils, Rabbi Eliezer and Rabbi Abba, collated his work into a book. This was the original *Book of Splendor*. For the next thousand years, the Kabbalah was only studied by a few in the greatest secrecy. In 1280, the *Book of Splendor* reappeared, featuring the corrections of Rabbi Moses de Leon from Spain.

Only after that did the Christians discover the Kabbalah and begin to study it.

The *Book of Splendor* actually consists of five books, the fifth of which deals with "the redemption of souls". "All the souls are subject to a sentence of assessment and spiritual change. Human beings do not know the master plan, they do not know that they are on trial all the time: before they come into this world, and when they leave it."

From Brussels to Bombay

Michel Coursier was born in Brussels and grew up there during the 1950s. The new Kokkelberg region was only about a half-hour from the city center. During his childhood years, he frequently went to the big and famous church there, despite his Jewish origins. The little boy was fascinated by the elegant building. All of the neighborhood children would play in the snow each winter; in the summer, they would chase the ducks in the small lake. In Michel's home, they spoke Flemish, French and English, and listened to classical music. When it was time for him to go to university, it seemed natural for him to opt for international relations.

Ten years later, when Michel was exactly thirty years old, he reached India for the first time. It was his first official mission. Some people were astonished that the Belgian government dared to send an unmarried official representative to a faraway country, but Michel was suitable and agreed to go on very short notice from the Foreign Office.

After two months of official meetings with the diplomatic staff there, Michel was finally free to spend a little time sightseeing in the environs. He would leave his house in the evening and go down to the River Ganges. There were always people there. At all hours of the day and night, there were people burning their dead, bathing, and doing their laundry.

Every few yards, he could see a different picture of Indian life with its caste system.

One evening, while he was strolling along the river as he always did, he noticed a young woman sitting on a large stone and playing a small flute. She was very young, thin and dark, and the most surprising thing was that she was playing a Flemish tune that Michel recognized from his childhood. The sharp contrast between the landscape and the tune moved him and brought tears to his eyes. Suddenly he felt very homesick. He decided that he would visit his homeland the following month and not wait for Christmas in three months' time. While he was thinking about home, the woman got up and came over to him. She looked at him with a penetrating gaze and held out her hand for charity. Michel, embarrassed, rummaged in his pockets and found nothing. "Come home with me, it's not far. I'll be able to give you a little money."

To his surprise, the woman, whose name was Rajin, answered him in English. She told him that she had spent her childhood in a local orphanage until she was adopted by an English immigrant couple who had come to live in Bombay in the 1960s. They taught her English as well as European music and culture, and treated her with love and warmth. However, when they both died of a mysterious disease within half a year of each other, she was left destitute.

Rajin went with Michel to his house. He gave her some food and money, and suggested that she return the next day so that he could try and help her find work. When she arrived at his house the next morning, she looked completely different. She was wearing an old but clean suit, her long black hair was carefully pulled back, and she looked European in every way except her dark skin. The phone rang. Michel's mother was calling to ask how he was and to tell him about the birth of her first grandchild - the son of his eldest sister. The conversation was in Flemish, and when it was over, Rajin said "Congratulations" in Flemish. They were both astounded. "I didn't know you spoke Flemish," said Michel. "Nor did I," was the reply.

It turned out that Rajin also knew how to read documents in Flemish even before anyone bothered to teach her the language in an orderly way. She could also talk about places she had never been to in her life. For instance, she could talk about the church where Michel had visited during his childhood, the chestnuts sold by old people during the winter, the little one-wheeled stalls. She could even talk about the only Scroll of the Law in the region that was in Michel's parents' home, and served as a focal point for Jews from all over the region during the High Holydays.

Treasure in a cave

Moshe was only 12, but he understood what was about to happen. Everyone was going to die. His father stood and sharpened the carving knife, the sharp knife he used for slaughtering chickens, even though there was not even one chicken left alive. His mother had been wandering around red-eyed since the early morning. She didn't know what was about to happen, but the atmosphere was heavy. Something terrible was looming and everyone felt it. The sentinels on the walls were standing and looking out at the Roman soldiers who were working hard and advancing toward Masada. It was a matter of one day. No more. No one really intended falling into the captivity of the hated Romans. Death was a certainty.

Moshe found himself running frantically to the home of his best friend, Avraham. "I'm running away," he informed him in a trembling voice. Moshe told Avraham his suspicions regarding what was about to happen. Avraham, who was only 13, cried like a baby. After a few long moments of hesitation, he agreed. When darkness fell, the two boys slid down a long rope outside the wall. They began to run like mad in order to get away as quickly as possible. The Roman soldiers, drunk with early victory, did not see the two figures slipping into the darkness of the night. In the morning, when the first soldiers reached the top of Masada, a ghastly silence greeted them. Everyone was dead...

Moshe and Avraham continued fleeing throughout the night. When dawn began to break, they saw a cave in the side of the mountain. They climbed up the cliff and squeezed into the small opening. Shaking with cold, terrified and grief-stricken for their families, they fell into a deep sleep. When they woke up later that day, they discovered three large clay jars next to the eastern wall of the cave. The first contained food. The two others contained gold coins and parchment scrolls. Avraham and Moshe rolled the jars into the depths of the cave. They also heaped a large pile of stones on and around the jars so that they could not be found. They swore to each other that they would return here when they had settled down. Their hope was that they would be able to reach the Jerusalem region and go to one of the small settlements in which the Romans were not in the least interested.

It was a matter of bad luck. A few hours after they had left the cave, they bumped into a shepherd who gave them a bit of food and water. They were filled with hope, but it turned out that their joy was premature. Toward evening of that same day, they ran into soldiers of the Roman legion. Death came too quickly for the two young boys. They died with the words "Hear O Israel" on their lips...

"Hear O Israel, the Lord our God, the Lord is one"... murmured David at the end of his morning prayers. Here, too, inside the walls of the Warsaw Ghetto, he had not given up the custom he had adopted when he was 13, when he became Bar Mitzvah. The daily morning prayer fortified him on good days and especially on difficult days. That overcast day, he burst into the office of the Gestapo officer and asked to speak to him privately.

The man with the fair hair and the cold blue eyes looked at the young kneeling Jew. The latter asked him to spare the lives of his baby son and his wife Hannah. "I have a lot of money," he told the officer...

Wilhelm Schultz recognized Hannah, the wife of the pleading Jew-boy. It was impossible not to notice her. Despite the harsh conditions, she stood out. She was the most beautiful woman in the ghetto, with long black hair and big green eyes. She was all of 20 years old, but spoke three languages, which had helped her to get a job in the ghetto offices. After Schultz had heard David out, he agreed to the deal. Hannah and her baby son's lives would be spared.

A month later, David was sent to the gas chamber. He was at peace when he died. Although he was not one hundred percent certain that the Nazi would keep his promise, he knew that for the time being, the lives of the people he loved above all were safe.

Schultz took Hannah home under the pretext of helping his ailing wife. Hannah, of course, brought her baby son Moshe with her. The year-old infant was tied to his mother's back throughout the day. In the evening, she would shut herself up with him in the little room she had been given and go to sleep early. One night, she heard a knock at the door. Schultz came into the room in his uniform and muddy black boots. "I'm sorry, your husband is dead," he told her. And then, much to her surprise, he pulled a small red apple from his pocket and handed it to her without saying another word. Hannah grabbed the apple. Schultz retraced his steps and went out of the room.

In 1958, the Nazi war criminal, Wilhelm Schultz, arrived in Israel. He had been living in Colombia under an assumed name since the end of World War II. He had arrived accompanied by his wife Hannah and his son Morgan Schultz. No one other than "the parents" knew that Morgan was in fact little Moshe who had been saved in the Warsaw Ghetto thanks to a small piece of paper and a package full of gold coins that his father had handed over to the Gestapo officer. Wilhelm's first wife and three children had been killed in an explosion in his car. The bomb had been meant for Schultz himself, but the hand of fate intervened so that on that particular day, he sent his driver on that fateful trip. Hannah and little Moshe were waiting for him in the big house after the funeral. Gradually, Hannah discovered Schultz's human side. He had been in love with her for a long time. Four more months went by, and one night Schultz, Hannah and little Moshe fled to Austria. From there, the way to South America was open.

Hannah and Schultz were married in a modest ceremony. They lived a quiet, peaceful life, accepting the cruel fate that had apparently thrown them together so that they could complete something that had remained unfinished from some long-ago time in the past...

When Hannah became ill with cancer, Schultz decided to immigrate to Israel. The medical treatment was only a pretext. He knew that he had to find closure. After they had settled down in a small apartment near the hospital, he set out to deal with the reason for which he had come to Israel.

He hired a car and loaded it with enough equipment for him and his son Morgan for a week in the Judean Desert. Only after they had arrived in the region, armed with maps, did he pull out the crumpled piece of paper he had kept for twenty years. He opened it with trembling hands. There, next to the campfire, he told Morgan for the first time the secret that David, Moshe's real father, had entrusted to him. The note, which had been passed from generation to generation, contained an ancient map of the Judean Desert with strange markings on it. Schultz also pulled out the one and only remaining coin - a gold coin that bore the portrait of an emperor.

At the end of the fifth day, Schultz and Morgan reached the cave... Morgan immediately knew where to look. He went up to the pile of stones and quickly dismantled it. A blow from a hammer... and a pile of gold coins with the emperor's portrait on them poured out on to the ground with a dull sound.

Hannah died at the end of that year - not before she knew that her son Morgan had found the lost treasure that her first husband, David, had told her about during the long cold winter nights so many years ago. She had always thought that it was a legend, the kind of legend that exists in every family. It turned out that truth was stranger than fiction. Morgan and Schultz had indeed discovered an amazing treasure.

Morgan took care of his adoptive father until the day he died. He even took the trouble to house him in a retirement home for people from Germany. There, Schultz sat and listened to the stories of the Holocaust survivors, some of whom had been in the concentration camp at the same time he was working there, but fortunately for him, they didn't recognize him.

Morgan became a very rich young man. As a result of the dramatic event that had occurred in his life at age 19, he decided to study archeology and Jewish history. Today he is a lecturer at one of the universities in Israel. His hobby is the subject of reincarnation.

Taoism

Before the revolutionary social and political changes that took place in China over recent years, one could say that every Chinese had a hat like that of Confucius, a garment like that of a Taoist, and sandals like those of Buddha. Many Chinese espoused the three religions, thereby making life difficult for researchers who tried to classify the different religious groups in the East.

While Confucius did not teach the subject of rebirth and eternal life, he did not deny it either. He focused on the social realm and ignored the mystical one. His mission was clear: he taught the masses how to behave and showed a great deal of respect for Lao-Tze, who was considered to be the founder of Taoism.

At age 35, Confucius traveled to meet the holy man Lao-Tze, who was turning 88 at the time. After the meeting, Confucius was so agitated and excited that he defined his feeling in the following words: "I saw a dragon."

Lao-Tze emerged in the world arena at the time of Buddha, Pythagoras, Ezekiel and Isaiah. The story of his life includes legends that are characteristic of heroes and great teachers who rose from humanity during the course of history. Like Jesus and Buddha, people related to his birth as a miracle, because his mother was a virgin, according to the sources. As a symbol of his great wisdom, there were people who said that he had emerged from his mother's womb with his face wreathed in a white beard.

Another myth about his external appearance concerned his long ears.

In this context, it is interesting to mention that most of the statues of Buddha also portray him with long ears. This may indicate a particularly great ability to listen to "the private I" or to "the voice of silence".

Lao-Tze is renowned and esteemed for his book, *The Tao of the I-Ching*. This book was declared to be a work of genius as early as the time of the emperor Ti, from the Han dynasty, prior to the birth of Jesus. The contents of the book were defined, among other things, as "a description of a transcendental method and a philosophy". The subject of eternal life is only mentioned in hints regarding people's return to the universe at regular intervals. Reincarnation is mentioned again, and more clearly, in a rewritten version of his writings by his pupil, Chong Tzu. Lao-Tze himself, according to the Taoist tradition, belonged to this religious stream in his previous incarnations: as the king Kwang Chang Tze during the period of the Yellow Emperor, and as Po-Chang during the period of Yao.

The following quotation comes from a translation of *The Tao of the I-Ching*:

"There is something that existed even before paradise and earth. This something is silent, stands before itself without changing, reaches every place, it is eternal. Its name I do not know. In order to define it, I will call it Tao. This is something that is difficult to define, to which all things return. It is not something visible, it is not audible, and it has no borders. It is infinite. The Tao creates all things, and nourishes them. Its nature gives them form, its strength perfects them. The Tao that can be expressed in words is not the eternal Tao. Without a name, it is a beginning of paradise and earth. When it is given a name, it becomes 'the mother of every living thing on the earth.'

"All things in nature work silently. They are created, but nothing really belongs to them.

"They fulfill their functions, without demanding a single thing. When the goal has been accomplished, do not take the glory for yourself, since if you do not do so – the thing will never be able to be taken away from you. He who is modest will remain whole. He who bends is the one who will straighten up. The empty will fill up. The worn out will be renewed. He who is aware of his own light, and is prepared to be out of the ordinary, will use his inner light in order to turn to the natural brightness. The large way is smooth."

A slope in China

A heavy fog lay along the winding mountain road that evening. Eighteen-year-old Weng Kiangi, elegantly dressed as befit her station, sat in a carriage pulled by two white horses. The carriage echoed along the descending road between Shanghai and Jiantzu. The driver held onto the reins tightly as the horses tried to find their way in the decreasing light. At one of the bends, the inevitable happened. The carriage plunged into the deep abyss. For a few minutes, the loud and terrible sound of the screams of pain issuing from man and beast was heard, and then silence reigned once more...

One hundred and ten years later, Doctor Jang Yan was traveling along exactly the same road. He was on his way to Jiantzu to visit his elderly parents, slowly driving his silver Mercedes and whistling a quiet tune to himself. Yan was very pleased with life, and he had every reason in the world to be pleased. At age 35, he was renowned throughout the country as a doctor, and wealthy to boot. Twice a year, he would visit the members of his family who had remained in the village. He never forgot where he came from and always made sure to bring them gifts and make them happy.

After a few hours of driving along the winding mountain road, Yan felt fatigue creeping up on him and taking control of him. He remembered that the previous night he had worked very hard and had slept for only two hours. The number of women giving birth broke all records: eight births one after the other. He was toying with the idea of whether it was a good idea to stop and rest at the side of the road, when there was suddenly a loud noise. A large bird had crashed into the windshield of the car. Shocked, Yan tried to press on the brake pedal, but pressed instead on the accelerator. The fancy car spun sharply and only stopped after it had crashed into a big rock at the side of the road. Yan was thrown 20 yards out of the car. He lay on the ground with blood pouring out of his head...

Luckily for Yan, someone was apparently looking out for him. A few minutes later, another car came along and quickly stopped at the sight of Yan's smashed car blocking the road. Two men and two young girls quickly got out of the commercial vehicle. Very carefully, they lifted Yan's body, placed it on the floor of the car and began to drive quickly to the nearest town. The village doctor, Kwan Chen, who had been summoned from his bed, recommended that the injured man be taken to a big hospital where he could receive the proper treatment. Late that night, a special ambulance from the Shanghai Municipal Hospital arrived to pick up the doctor, who was loved and admired by everyone. Many of the members of the medical team shed a tear when the ambulance brought Yan to the intensive care unit...

For four months, Dr. Yan lay in a coma. His relatives were summoned to his bedside, where they tried to speak to him and play him his favorite childhood songs endlessly - but to no avail. One morning, without any warning, while his old mother was sitting exhausted next to his bed, Yan suddenly opened his eyes and said: "Weng Kiangi". His excited mother called the doctor on duty and the relatives in the adjoining room. No one knew exactly what Yan meant. He said nothing more. It was none other than the old cleaning man who came to the rescue when he entered the room at a certain point in order to clean it. According to him, there was an old legend about Weng Kiangi, a young, beautiful girl who had been killed in a terrible road accident along with the driver of her carriage on the road from Shangai to Jiangtzu.

Within a few days, Yan's condition had improved beyond recognition. He became his old self almost entirely, and began to eat and talk. After three more months of various treatments, he was completely back on his feet. The only residual problem was a lack of sensation in his right foot. All that time, Weng Kiangi's name did not stop bothering him. The name came back to him in dreams, and when he was awake, he would hear a young woman's voice calling him...

Yan decided to seek the help of a well-known medium in order to try to find out what it meant. What later transpired did not surprise him at all. Some research recommended by the medium revealed beyond a doubt that the driver who had driven Weng Kiangi to her death was Yan's relative. It also turned out that after the death of the girl, her grief-stricken mother had hanged herself and her father had committed suicide by drinking poison. The remaining younger children were scattered among various orphanages.

After these facts came to light, Yan knew exactly what he had to do. He spent a few days locating Weng Kiangi's family in one of the poor neighborhoods of Shanghai. When he arrived there in the new black car he had purchased, all the people in the neighborhood were astonished to see an important and wealthy man in such a place. The members of Weng Kiangi's family were surprised to hear that the senior doctor from the hospital had decided to take them under his wing and provide them with everything they needed. The first sum of money he gave them was used to renovate the modest house that belonged to Weng Kiangi's relatives. The second - larger - sum was used for opening a small grocery store.

Two months later, Yan led a special team along the mountain road. With the help of a crane, the remains of Weng and the driver were lifted from the abyss and buried with full honors in a cemetery in Shanghai. That same day, after the double funeral, the sensation returned to Yan's right foot. He had come full circle.

Back to Japan

Sakuri Ya was the eldest daughter born to a rich and important family in a small village that nestled at the foot of the threatening Mount Fujiyama. At a young age, it was obvious that she was different than the other little girls. While the others hid under their mothers' aprons, she preferred to spend hours outdoors, sitting silently in front of a blooming cherry tree or observing Mount Fujiyama with its eternally snowy peak. By the time Ya turned 18, it was clear that she was not going to settle down and have a family. She declared that she wanted to be a *miko* - a spiritual teacher and doctor. Her mother spent the night weeping. She knew her daughter would lead a hard and solitary life, devoid of the children that constitute the essence of the Japanese woman's existence.

After a sleepless night, Ya and her mother rose early in the morning. The two packed a bit of equipment in a small cloth bag and Ya walked along the snowy path to the nearby hill at the isolated edge of the village.

For a week, she underwent a series of rituals including pouring icy water on her naked body, prayer, and focusing on nature. After the seven days, she returned pale and famished to her parents' home. She had passed all the tests and had become the official "miko" of the village.

For many years, Ya healed sick people in the village and held secret rituals during which spirits from the past appeared and told their stories... She wrote everything down in a flowing hand in a large black notebook in which, in addition to prescriptions for medications and secret potions, she also wrote down a prophecy: "The day will come when a white man with yellow hair will come down the mountain. The foreign man will be a miko for you..."

After Ya's death, the big black notebook was passed on from one generation of miko to the next, in a large wooden box in which remedial herbs and various amulets were also kept. Three hundred years later, Ya's prophecy came true.

Micha Sharir from U.S.A reached the small village at the foot of Mount Fujiyama. He had been born in a small agricultural settlement in a desert. His only memories of his childhood were the low yellow hills that stretched to the horizon, the dusty winds and the small workshop of his father, who worked as an ironmonger. Inga, Micha's mother, was a music teacher and found it very difficult to find work in the immediate surroundings, so she would travel to the city twice a week, and stay over at the house of her friend.

As a lonely child whose parents and brother - a soldier who came home infrequently - did not pay much attention to him, Micha began to spend most of his free time painting. At age six, he began to paint mountains of all sizes and shapes. However, what they all had in common was their snowy peak.

It was only two years later, when the drawers in his room overflowed with paintings, that his parents discovered that their child was tremendously gifted. They immediately registered him in an art class, and afterwards, when the time came for him to go to high school, he majored in art, of course. When he went on to study at a College of Art, he continued painting enchanted landscapes, snowy mountains and blooming cherry trees. No one knew where the youngster who had grown up in the arid desert got the inspiration for his paintings.

After he graduated cum laude from college, Micha wanted to take a trip to the Far East.

The Boeing landed at the Osaka airport one bright spring morning. Micha took a cab without knowing where he wanted to go. He wanted to get an impression of the surroundings before checking in at a hotel. The driver suggested that they go to a small village near Nomazu. When they reached the village, the cab driver's elderly mother invited them to a typical Japanese meal.

Sitting on a mat on the floor near the open window, Micha realized that he was looking at the landscapes he had painted all his life. Right in front of him, like a magic wand, through a veil of fine mist, Mount Fujiyama with its snowy peak was gazing at him in all its glory. Micha finished eating and asked the old lady if he could rent a room in the enchanted village and spend a few days there. She looked at him with a penetrating stare and muttered something quickly to her son, the cab driver. The latter bowed respectfully and left the room hurriedly. An hour later, he returned with an old woman leaning on a stick. Under her arm she carried a carved wooden box decorated with golden characters. This she handed to Micha with trembling hands...

Micha stayed in the village. According to the explanations of his new friend, the cab driver, he understood that he was apparently the person whom Ya, the village *miko*, had expected 300 years ago. Micha sent a single letter to his parents in the small settlement, announcing that he was not coming back. There was simply no point in explaining. A few months later, Micha began to speak the local language. Immediately after that, the people of the village began to call him "*miko*". He was one of them and everyone knew it.

Fresh chicken

From a very young age, Gila hated eating meat. The kitchen in the little apartment was small and crowded, and the smell of the food on the little table made her feel nauseous. Occasionally, Gila's mother would give in and allow her to eat in her room while reading.

It all began one day when Gila's father brought some chickens from the market and her mother stood in the kitchen and singed the feathers. The smell of the dead chickens and the burned feathers was pungent and revolting. The gas flames burned blue. For no apparent reason, the six-year-old Gila was overcome with an attack of hysterical crying followed by a wave of vomiting that went on all night. The next day, she got up with a burning rash all over her body. Her frightened mother sat her in a large basin and washed her small body with pink kali water.

A few hours later, since there was no improvement in her condition, they all went to the family doctor. Doctor Weiner took one look at the child whose eyes swollen from crying, heard the facts and wrote a prescription for a white ointment with a strong odor. The rash disappeared. Daddy didn't bring any more fresh chickens from the market.

Eight years went by. When she was 14, she began to study the history of Spanish Inquisition at school. Her discomfort was replaced by a feeling of horror when the details began to mount up. The stories of the torture suffered ... Gila stopped participating in the lessons, did not do her homework and would wake up screaming at night.

Her worried parents consulted Dr. Yehuda Fogel, who was renowned as a "psychiatrist with a soul" and excelled in working with children. The elderly doctor had a white beard and forelock. His room smelled pleasantly of tobacco, and its walls were full of shelves piled with books. After an introductory conversation, Dr. Fogel suggested to Gila and her parents that Gila try hypnosis in order to find out the meaning of the dreams and the nightmares that she had been having incessantly for weeks. After 20 sessions, the doctor summoned Gila and her parents. His face was serious when he explained that the tape he was holding contained the things Gila had said while under hypnosis. He suggested that they all listen to it, even though it was particularly unpleasant. "Only after you understand what the reason is will the road to recovery begin..."

The words were repeated over and over again. There was no room for error. "I am running in an open field in a long black dress, barefoot and terrified. Five priests are running after me. They are chasing me and I don't know why. They are wearing long robes with a rope tied around their waists. On each priest's chest swings a thick chain with a large cross hanging from it. In spite of the darkness, I can see the way. The moon is full and it lights up the path that leads to a graveyard. Puffing and panting, I reach the graveyard, trying to think why I'm actually fleeing and who my pursuers are. I wipe the sweat that is dripping into my eyes with the back of my hand, push my long black hair back and run faster. My efforts don't help. Gradually I feel my strength decreasing. I don't have much left. Another minute and another minute, and then a hand shoots out and grabs my shoulder. I hear them breathing heavily. My heart stops beating for a moment. When the fat priest with the cross throws me on to the cold ground, I understand that my end has come. The hunt is over. For them, however, the fun has just begun."

Gila's parents were stunned. The rest of the tape was no easier to listen to. They heard their daughter telling how the first priest, who dragged her between the trees, was tall and strong, with dark hair and eyes gleaming with hatred. He leaned over her and she smelled his sour sweat. He pinned her to the ground and forced her legs open. She screamed in agony as he penetrated her. The act was repeated with the other priests. At this point, Gila lost consciousness only to wake up the next morning in the cellars of the Inquisition, with other who were about to be burned at the stake. In a small, gray cell in which rats and mice scuttled around freely, Gila waited for a week, injured, hurting, on the brink of madness. After the High Inquisitor himself signed the necessary documents, 200 Jews were burned at the stake on a single day in the city of Valencia. The screams of the doomed mingled with the yells of the roaring masses that were waiting to see the hated Jews burn to death. The last thing Gila remembered was the smell of her burning flesh and the terrible pain. Then everything went black.

Pale and silent, Gila and her parents sat for several long minutes after the tape ended. There was not much to explain. What Gila had gone through in her previous incarnation had come back and overwhelmed her every time something happened in her daily life - even a hint - to remind her of the events that had occurred in the past.

Gila attended a few more sessions with Dr. Fogel. He helped

her to digest the things that had risen to the surface. She learned to live with them. However, even today, years after it all happened, on Lag Be'Omer [a Jewish festival in which bonfires are lit], when the smell of the bonfires permeates the air, Gila suffers from an attack of unease. She closes the shutters and turns the radio on full blast...

Dark red

Frieda stood and looked at the sea. She always stood in the same place wearing a red dress. She was a familiar and popular figure among the girls who worked in the street. A whore and a lady. You could rely on her, ask for her help, and even borrow money from her. She had only behaved violently once. It was at the beginning of her career, when she had just arrived on the scene and Jacko the pimp tried to threaten her and extort money from her. She pulled out a knife and held it at his throat with a fast and skilled movement. From that day on, no one bothered her.

One Friday, in the summer of 1982, the sun was high in the sky. It was very hot. Frieda was assailed by a feeling of restlessness and a gloomy mood. She took off her red spike-heeled sandals and went down barefoot to the beach.

Suddenly she heard a familiar voice asking her in English: "Will you come with me?" She turned round and found herself looking at a completely strange face. The man standing opposite her had fair hair and penetrating blue eyes. As if hypnotized, she followed him up to the 17th floor of the Hotel. There, in the luxury suite, he ordered room service.

They sat for an hour while he told her that he had come from a large ranch in Texas. He said that one night he had dreamed that he had to come to this place in order to find the person who would be his wife. The strange dream, he said, had recurred several times and he had decided to try.

Frieda went down in the hotel elevator only after spending two days with the tall stranger. They both felt that their meeting had been pre-ordained. She returned that same evening with a small suitcase full of clothes, and then the two of them went off for a break in a hotel where no one knew her. Another ten days passed, and they knew that they would remain together for always.

They took a large, white cab to the home of Frieda's parents in a small, neglected town in the south of the country. Two hours later, they traveled directly to the airport and got on to the huge Jumbo jet that was leaving for Texas. Frieda and Tom arrived in Texas on a hot summer night. She immediately felt at home, and even the landscape seemed familiar to her. They had a modest wedding there, and Tom's relatives could not conceal their admiration for the beautiful woman Tom had brought back.

Two years went by. Frieda and Tom became the parents of twin boys called Steve and John. Frieda and Tom were happy. His meat business was thriving. She lived a comfortable life, spending most of her free time with her new friends. During the third year, Frieda and Tom went on vacation to the family's summer house in a region where there was a large lake.

One day, while Tom was out fishing and the twins were sleeping, Frieda went into the spacious library and pulled out a big, heavy book that had attracted her attention for some reason. A photograph and a yellowing piece of paper slipped out from between its pages. Frieda's heart missed a beat. She glanced at the photo and was astonished to discover that the woman in it looked exactly like her. She was wearing a red velvet dress, and at her side there was a tall, blond man sporting a broad-brimmed gray hat. On the back of the photo was written: Samantha and Andy McCartney. On the piece of paper, in the delicate handwriting of a young girl, was a love poem to the man she loved who had saved her from a wasted life in Bertha's brothel.

When Tom returned that evening with a basket full of fish, she hurried to show him the treasure she had found. As soon as they returned home, Tom showed the photo and the poem to his embarrassed parents, who were unable to provide him with any information about the matter, except the fact that there was no doubt that the people in the photo were relatives.

After three more months of amateur "detective work", Frieda got on a plane to New York, having made an appointment with the well-known hypnotist, Michael Kewley, beforehand. After he heard the story, the hypnotist promised to find out whatever he could.

The next day, during their second session, he already had a document confirming that the two people in the photo had lived about a century ago in a small village in the western United States. During the course of the session, the convoluted link between the picture in the old library, whose existence no one remembered, and her own life. Samantha McCartney was a tall, impressive girl. Her blonde hair shone and was arranged in flowing curls, as was the fashion at that time. She always wore high-quality red velvet dresses decorated with shiny beads. She would paint her sensual lips shiny red and made sure to powder her turned-up nose so that it wouldn't shine. It was not surprising that Samantha became the favorite of the clients at Bertha's brothel. Her name was known throughout the Wild West. They called her "the girl in red". Although four years on the job is a long time, Samantha preserved her grace and innocence, attributes that were not characteristic of working girls. One day, when the temperature outside turned the street into a furnace, the door opened. In a white cloud of dust stood a tall, handsome man with penetrating blue eyes. Like a viper hypnotizing its prey, his eyes roved over the girls who were lying exhausted on the couches. Samantha knew that he would choose her even before he lifted his hand, which was adorned with a heavy gold ring, and pointed at her...

They went up to her room and made love for an hour. He held her in his arms until dawn broke. The next day, without saying goodbye to anyone, Samantha packed a small bundle of clothes and the two went off on horseback, over the hill, never to return.

The fourteenth Dalai Lama

Among believers, every Dalai Lama is an incarnation of his predecessor. It is claimed that "the Dalai Lama is an exceptional person in every way, rare and unique. He is wise and educated, but possesses childlike traits. He is with you, and at the same time detached. He evokes feelings of love, and, in parallel, something else."

The present Dalai Lama was declared to be the last incarnation of the Dalai Lama dynasty at age two and a half. Among other things, it is written about the sequence of events that the previous Dalai Lama had a vision featuring three letters, a monastery with a green and gold roof, and a house whose floor was made of turquoise tiles.

A precise description of the vision was written down and concealed in a safe place. When the Tibetan sages traveled throughout the land seeking an infant that was supposed to be the incarnation of the Dalai Lama, they reached a village called Takaster in the Amdu province in northeastern Tibet. In a house whose floor was made of turquoise tiles, next to a monastery with a green and gold roof, they found the heir.

The true test, of course, was whether the child could recognize and remember different people who were linked to his previous life. To this end, the leader of the group of sages dressed up as a simple servant and entered the house with the turquoise floor.

The parents, who suspected nothing, invited the man into the kitchen, where the two-year-old child was playing. The esteemed sage wore a chain belonging to the thirteenth Dalai Lama around his neck. The child immediately asked for it.

Surprised but alert, the man promised the child that he would give him the chain if he knew his name. The child immediately answered: "Saraga", which meant, in the local dialect, "Lama of Balasa Monastery". Subsequently, he picked out personal objects that had belonged to the Dalai Lama from a large pile of items.

Jack London (1876-1916), the American novelist, was extremely interested in reincarnation, and some of his novels are filled with his views on the topic. *The Star Rover* is one of them:

All my life I have had an awareness of other times, and places. I have been aware of other persons in me. ... I, whose lips had never lisped the word "king," remembered that I had once been the son of a king. More – I remembered that once I had been a slave and a son of a slave, and worn an iron collar round my neck.

I, like any man, am a growth. I did not begin when I was born, nor when I was conceived. I have been growing, developing, through incalculable myriads of millenniums. All these experiences of all these lives, have gone to the making of the soul-stuff or the spirit-stuff that is I. ... I am all of my past, as every protagonist of the Mendelian law must agree. All my previous selves have their voices, echoes, promptings in me. ... I am man born of woman. My days are few, but the stuff of me is indestructible. I have been woman born of woman. I have been a woman and borne my children. And I shall be born again. Oh, incalculable times again shall I be born; and yet the stupid dolts about me think that by stretching my neck with a rope they will make me cease.

J. London, *The Star Rover*

On the bank of the river

Corona Adams lived alone in a small studio apartment in Oregon in the United States. At age 28, single and very lonely, she felt that she wanted to run away from everything and everybody. Her work as a schoolteacher bored her, she was tired of her aging parents and her noisy neighbors...

She leafed impatiently through the pages of the newspaper with her eyes racing back and forth. Suddenly her eye fell on a small ad:

"Wanted - an English teacher for work on a ship..."

Four weeks later, Corona found herself on board a large naval boat that was sailing to the island of Diego Garcia. She had never heard of the place prior to being told that it was located slightly south of the equator in the heart of the Indian Ocean. Her job was to stay with the soldiers on the island for six months and to give them enrichment lessons in English. Everything happened very fast, but for the first time in years, Corona felt that her hasty decision was one hundred percent correct for her.

When they reached the island, she was astounded at the harsh conditions of heat and climate, but at the same time, could not deny her powerful feeling of *déjà vu*. She felt as if she knew every corner, every tree, every curve in the coastline. At night, when she couldn't sleep, she would go walking along the dark shores, listening to the whispering sound of the waves crashing on the shore. She spent most of her free time with Zina Clinton, the only American girl on the ship and the commander's secretary. One evening, when she told Zina about her feelings regarding the island, she was surprised to see her friend's face becoming serious. "I feel the same thing," she confessed. "Exactly as if I lived here once."

On their first day off, the two got dressed in pants and long shirts and equipped themselves with a few useful tools: a large knife, two hoes, a hammer, water, and a little food. They left the ship in a small rowboat, left it tied to a palm tree on the shore, and made their way into the thick tropical jungle. After an exhausting trek of about four hours among screaming monkeys, gigantic mosquitoes and butterflies, they reached the bank of a river.

Corona Adams sat down on a big stone. Zina froze on the spot for a moment, pointed at the stone with a trembling hand, and said: "It's here."

With their combined strength, the two women managed to roll the heavy stone to one side. They began to dig like people possessed, beating the moist earth with their small hoes, and casting aside the long black worms that appeared among the clods of earth.

After what seemed like an eternity, they pulled an old rotting wooden box out of the hole. The rusty lock yielded with one blow. Through the moss and the shreds of silk fabric, they saw a large pile of gold coins in the box. Corona and Zina shared the loot out equally.

They loaded up their backpacks and made their way back through the forest to the beach and from there to the ship. Six

months later, they returned to the United States and kept in touch for years.

In 1990, Corona and Zina were widowed. They both had grown children and decided to spend their remaining years together. They moved into a prestigious retirement home in Beverly Hills where they would tell anyone who was willing to listen the fantastic story of the treasure that had waited so many years for them in the tropical forest of Diego Garcia.

A trip to Mongolia

Kirk Grainer was one of the five scientists who went out to the Gobi Desert in Mongolia in 1922. The group had set itself the goal of finding ancient fossils. Among the participants was Yvette Andrews, Kirk's girlfriend.

The convoy of camels advanced slowly, with the foremost rider holding the American flag on a long thin stick.

When they reached the town of Orga, they encountered a Buddhist festival. Yvette and Kirk were not the only ones who were amazed at the celebrations. The abundance of bells, the colorful clothing and the monotonous music were familiar, for some reason, even though this was the first visit of all the participants to this godforsaken part of the world. After an exhausting journey in burning heat that seemed to go on forever, they reached their destination - the Gobi Desert. For 20 blazing days they traveled among the huge colorful cliffs that were 75 million years old. Initially, they still encountered local inhabitants who would appear out of nowhere and disappear again. From them they adopted the custom of covering their heads with lengths of fabric twisted like a scarf in order to maintain a certain degree of coolness and to shade their faces. Every day they found more and more fossils. There was an unending treasure trove of fossils and remains of rare animals. Kirk and Yvette simply knew which cliff to look behind and where to check the ground.

Other people who tried their luck did not succeed. After the first four days, everyone realized that it was worth their while leaving the task of primary location to Kirk and Yvette. In fact, what was happening was more astonishing than the team members could imagine.

Night after night, Kirk and Yvette would go to sleep in the tent they had erected, with pens and paper available at the heads of their camp beds. From the first night, they began to have dreams that seemed to be complementary. The first time they told each other about the events of the night, they were so excited that it was difficult for them not to share their discovery with the rest of the group. Eventually, however, they decided to refrain from doing so. Yvette dreamed that she was in a large cave, sitting next to a campfire. There were children and other women there. It took her a little time to notice that they were all wearing skins and furs. She identified herself despite the fact that she looked very different than the figure that was reflected in the mirror. However, this was mainly because of the clothes and her facial expressions. She knew for certain that she was seeing herself in another, previous, life, when she held an important position in the small tribe. At night, when everyone went to sleep, she would sit and stir various mixtures in small clay bowls, some of which were used for the large cave paintings the women painted. Other mixtures were used for spreading on the men's bodies before they went hunting, or on the feverish foreheads of sick children. Every night, the men would return with the animals they had hunted during the day. The women would help them strip the skins off the carcasses and skewer the meat on long, sharp sticks that they suspended over the ever-burning fire. The odor of the roasting meat was so real that Yvette woke up. She got up, amazed, and boiled a little water on the small gas burner.

Afterwards, she made herself something to eat and went back to sleep next to Kirk. She noticed that he was moving back and forth restlessly and made a mental note to ask him what he had dreamed about next morning...

During breakfast, she began to tell him about the strange dream she had had that night, and then she saw that he had become pale. She kept quiet...

He continued from the place that she had left off. He told her about the cave, about the women waiting for the men and even about the cave paintings that she had not bothered to mention to him.

It seemed that the joint dreams were describing a different period of life, an ancient one, during which they were both partners and lived in the same place. During the course of the days they went out on sorties. Yvette and Kirk knew where to find fossils of Titanosaurus and Baluchisaurus teeth. The latter was a creature that was eight yards long and weighed 33 tons. Repeated tests measured the age of the fossils at 32 million years.

Initially, Kirk and Yvette did not relate to the dreams overly seriously. They attributed their luck in finding fossils to chance. They didn't try to explain the dreams. However, what happened three days prior to the end of the mission convinced them that they had indeed been here once. It was not the hand of chance that brought them back to the place where they knew every bit of land. They had been here and they returned here in order to give modern man the knowledge that was buried beneath the earth...

That day, Kirk and Yvette went off on a reconnaissance trip in their dusty blue jeep. They drove around the barren hills for hours without finding anything. Suddenly Yvette said: "Turn right and stop." They stopped at the edge of a high cliff beneath which lay an enormous abyss. A large stone that stood at the edge concealed a small black opening in the earth. With the shovels they had with them, Kirk and Yvette broadened the opening and slid inside using ropes. They found themselves standing in a large hall illuminated by rays of sunshine that shone through tiny holes in the rock ceiling. Yvette turned on her flashlight and advanced. Suddenly, she saw the cave paintings she had dreamed about the last few nights on the wall in front of her. When Kirk drew up next to her, she could hear his sharp intake of breath and she knew that he was not seeing the cave paintings for the first time. They were both familiar with the place from their dreams. The paintings were special and different from what they had ever seen or read about in books. This was the best proof of the fact that they could not have invented the whole thing even if they'd wanted to. As scientists, it was important for them to know that they were primary eyewitnesses. Undoubtedly, the discovery of the cave had also been helped along by the hand of fate. Kirk and Yvette, on their part, felt that after tens of millions of years, they had simply come home.

Mud trap

Alfredo Salvador dug among the ruins of his house in a desperate attempt to salvage something that had not been destroyed in the terrible hurricane. His wife and three-year-old son had perished. They were among the 7,000 people who had died in the largest natural disaster to befall Honduras in 1998. The tears Alfredo wept the night everything happened had already dried up. He had simply known that it was going to happen.

Alfredo had grown up on the banks of the Rio Choluteca, the river that had once swallowed up his little brother Ricardo. He was three when he died, and Alfredo had never forgotten how his mother had wept when it happened 20 years ago. Rena Francisca, Alfredo's mother, was a young widow who had been left with five children and the burden of supporting them after her husband Jorge had been killed in the capital city, Tegucigalpa, when he fell off the scaffolding of a building where he was working. He did not have a trade and was therefore obliged to work at odd jobs. The little money he earned he sent to his wife in the small village so that she and the children would have something to eat. He wanted to prevent his children from having the same fate as the thousands of children who lived in the streets of the big city...

After his father's death, which occurred when Alfredo was only 15 years old, he himself went to the big city in order to take his dead father's place. He rummaged through the garbage cans of fancy restaurants, earned a living by cleaning the windows of the wealthy diners' luxury cars, and lived in a cardboard box in the huge city garbage dump, along with many other homeless comrades. Four years later, he returned home after his mother found work in one of the big coffee plantations in the region. Alfredo also looked for work. Fortune smiled upon him, and he was accepted for agricultural work in one of the packing plants that belonged to a rich man who, unlike his heartless counterparts, tried to give his workers a little food in addition to the pittance he paid them. A year later, there was a flood. The only survivors were Alfredo and his eldest sister.

Two more years passed and Alfredo met the woman who became his wife. He begged Roberta to leave the place where he had known so much death and bereavement, but she refused. When their first son was born, Alfredo wept all night. A terrible premonition haunted him the whole week. The feeling augmented when his wife suggested that they call the new baby Ricardo. He pleaded with her to change the name, but to no avail. They lived in a hut in the village and tried to live as well as they could on the meager means they had at their disposal. Alfredo continued working in the packing plant. When the baby was three months old, Roberta, entrusted the new baby to her mother and returned to her job of cutting sugar cane. The bigger Ricardo grew, the more he resembled Alfredo's little brother. He loved doing the same things and was also in the habit of calling his father by the strange name "Illi", just as little Ricardo had done before he died.

Alfredo believed in reincarnation. He was absolutely certain that the soul of his young brother had been reborn in the body of his young son. He was happy about this, but could never shake off the terrible feeling that had plagued him since the birth of his son.

Two months before the big flood, Alfredo began to suffer from nightmares again. These worsened relentlessly. A week before the flood, Alfredo began to weep every evening. After an exhausting day's work, sitting at the table that contained no food, he would sit and watch his wife putting the child to sleep despite the fact that he was crying with hunger. The little green melons Alfredo brought home gave them nothing but stomach-aches, and besides the single loaf of bread that had to last them five days, they could get hold of almost nothing else to eat.

Three days later, Alfredo decided to do something. He went out of the village and hitched a ride to the big city of Tegucigalpa. Two more days passed until he managed to find work in one of the restaurants in the city. It was a stroke of luck and he was happy. Finally he would be able to send money to his family and even save a little in order to send for them in a few months' time.

Later that night, huge amounts of water flooded the village. Little Ricardo and his mother, along with thousands of other people, were buried beneath tons of slippery mud. Miraculously, Alfredo had survived, but his life was over. He returned to the village to look for his house and see what was left of it. After squatting among the ruins for two days, he got up and walked slowly to the banks of the river... Another nameless victim joined the long list of the dead...

What determines why a person is born into particular surroundings –
Swami Bakta Vishta

One person is born into a life of deprivation and suffering and is blessed with only a few abilities – and it seems as if he is predestined for a wretched life. Another person is born into the best surroundings and is nurtured and cared for by the best hands and hearts. From the beginning, he displays signs of extremely valuable talents. It is almost sure that his career will be a success story. Those who do not know better would say that the one was born lucky and the other was born unlucky.

However, anyone who studies nature knows that nothing happens by chance, and every effect must have a cause. As a rule, people imagine that talents and abilities are "inherited" from a certain branch of the family, and there is sufficient so-called proof to convince almost everyone that that is a fact. Ostensibly, the many books that have been written about heredity prove this beyond a doubt.

Even so, in spite of all the so-called proof, I claim that the events in which the person himself took part are responsible for creating his talents and abilities, and he does not owe the latter to the heritage of his forefathers. The person today is the result of what he was and did in the past.

There is something in the person himself that determines why he is born into particular surroundings, just as certain flowers must be planted in certain places so that they can thrive and bloom. An alpine flower, for instance, will not grow in the desert sand. Likewise, there is something in the person that determines why he is born into particular surroundings.

If you examine the person thoroughly, you will discover that he has an inner life that incessantly attempts to express itself. It cannot be passed on by heredity, and its source must be in previous lives – and now it wants to be expressed.

Parents are not begetters in the full sense of the word. They are a means that provides the organic material. When a soul enters another physical existence in this world, the temperament, nature and inclinations of the parents are known in advance. For this reason, the children reflect the particular combination of the parents' properties. Parents cannot create the true absolute center of any personality, nor do they possess the power to disrupt its development.

"Every person has already existed in everything to do with the basic form of his soul, since from the spiritual point of view, no person is identical to another person."

The forces that shape a particular existence are the result of the factors that existed in its previous life. If there were truth in the concept heredity, it would mean that every time an infant was born, a new personality would be formed. We would not have such a fierce desire to express our innermost and most secret existence. Without our innermost existence, and if we were first created when we opened our eyes on the world, life would seem alien and strange to us – and this is not the case. When an infant is born, he does not begin his life here for the first time.

The mistakes of the previous life combine with the person's spiritual cell, and the soil of the soul in which he finds himself, between death and new life, is the place in which the fruit ripens. Those are the talents and abilities that will appear in the new life and shape the personality so that it will appear as the result of what was attained in the previous life. Life becomes comprehensible to everyone when they try to understand what was said above. Of course it is impossible to believe in all the theories unless it is possible to experience some of them. My objective up until now has only been to present the facts, as the Prophet sees them, in an intelligent way. I want you to acquire personal knowledge about the spiritual facts that have been mentioned. The Prophet will never ask you to agree with any statement before you have verified it. Life does not become comprehensible until we acknowledge that these experiences are authentic.

Something occurs that causes the person a great deal of pain. He can see this in two ways: He can think only about the pain that he has been caused, and in this way he will not derive much benefit from the experience. Alternatively, he can say: "I am the one who in a previous life activated the power that caused me to have this experience. In effect, I brought it on myself." Thus he can turn this experience into a useful experience, because it helps him live a life in which he will not have to undergo a similar experience. If he stops and devotes some thought to the topic, what will happen will imprint a stamp on his consciousness that will help him refrain from doing certain deeds that he would otherwise have done.

No one can deny the fact that "forewarned is forearmed". If a person knows that in a previous life he activated the power within him that caused him to experience a certain event, he does not sit passively by while it is happening and blame his ill fortune. On the contrary, he knows that he is getting what he deserves, and therefore musters his strength and copes with the event in a different way than the way he would have done had he thought that this was mere chance and nothing more. He knows that the event that he would otherwise have related to as chance, was necessary, and sees it in that light. He learns to consider all these experiences as necessary experiences, derives benefit from them – and gradually they affect his life to a large extent. They assist his development amazingly. He learns the purpose of life, he learns the secret of his existence – the continuity of life. If he would only devote some thought to the life between birth and death, he would see it as an illusion.

No one can give you this inner knowledge, but everyone can learn it. Anyone who never knew of its existence cannot understand how convincing the proof is. Anyone who has become aware of it does not need anyone else to prove its existence to him. Each person must have the experience himself. The path is open to everyone.

More about Egypt

The history and culture of ancient Egypt have always fascinated many people. We are all enchanted by the pyramids, the sphynxes and the temples, as well as by the work, *The Book of the Dead.*

A writer by the name of Edna Faber wrote her autobiography entitled *Dubious Treasure* because she remembered nightmares from her childhood that were linked to the noise of carriage wheels. In her opinion, these vague memories were somehow linked to Egypt.

In order to examine the phenomenon, she went to Egypt, and later wrote a book, which also became a musical, whose plot takes place on the banks of the Nile. Her broad knowledge of the foreign country and of the great river that flows through it impressed other people and astonished her as well.

Herodotus, Plato, Plutarch and other ancient writers spoke about reincarnation as a general belief that prevailed among the Egyptians. Some people assume that this belief reached Egypt via Persia during the period it conquered and ruled Egypt.

Dr. Margaret Marais, who spent many years investigating Egyptian culture, cleaimed that this belief prevailed in Egypt long before the Persians arrived on the scene. She wrote a book called *The Splendor of Egypt* in which she claimed that reincarnation was an accepted and basic belief in ancient Egypt. She provide evidence for her claim by comparing the names of kings from the dynasty, meaning: rebirth.

The invention of the theory of reincarnation is attributed to

Pythagoras, even though many people think that the origin of the idea in Egypt is even more ancient.

In his book, *The Most Ancient Books in the World*, Meyer Isaac wrote: "Life on earth, from the point of view of the ancient Egyptians, constituted only a preparation for the next stage. The duration of existence was considered to be eternal, it began long before birth, and it continued long after the death of the physical body."

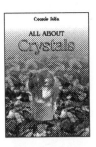

ALL ABOUT CRYSTALS
Connie Islin
ISBN 965-494-111-2

ALL ABOUT TAROT
Hali Morag
ISBN 965-494-062-0

**ALL ABOUT THE WICCA
OF LOVE**
Tabatha Jennings
ISBN 965-494-110-4

**ALL ABOUT THE SIXTH
SENSE**
Tom Pearson
ISBN 965-494-138-4

ALL ABOUT NUMEROLOGY
Lia Robin
ISBN 965-494-109-0

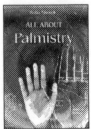

ALL ABOUT PALMISTRY
Batia Shorek
ISBN 965-494-094-9

ALL ABOUT DREAMS
Eili Goldberg
ISBN 965-494-061-2

**ALL ABOUT PREDICTING
THE FUTURE**
Sarah Zehavi
ISBN 965-494-093-0

ALL ABOUT SYMBOLS
Andrew T. Cummings
ISBN 965-494-139-2

ALL ABOUT CHAKRAS
Lily Rooman
ISBN 965-494-149-X